MW01031320

THE PRACTICAL PARENT

THE
PRACTICAL PARENT

ABCs of Child Discipline

Raymond J. Corsini and
Genevieve Painter

1817

HARPER & ROW, PUBLISHERS

New York   Evanston   San Francisco   London

Portions of this work originally appeared in *Family Circle*.

THE PRACTICAL PARENT. Copyright © 1975 by Raymond J. Corsini and Genevieve Painter. All rights reserved. Printed in the United States of America. No part of this book may be used or reproduced in any manner whatsoever without written permission except in the case of brief quotations embodied in critical articles and reviews. For information address Harper & Row, Publishers, Inc., 10 East 53rd Street, New York, N.Y. 10022. Published simultaneously in Canada by Fitzhenry & Whiteside Limited, Toronto.

FIRST EDITION

Designed by Patricia Dunbar

Library of Congress Cataloging in Publication Data

Corsini, Raymond J.
   The practical parent.
   Bibliography: p.
   Includes index.
   1. Children—Management. 2. Child study. 3. Discipline of children.
I. Painter, Genevieve, joint author. II. Title.
HQ769.C744   649'.1   74-1801
ISBN 0-06-010873-8

To the memory of our teacher,
Dr. Rudolf Dreikurs (1897–1971)

Contents

PART VII. HELPING OTHER FAMILIES

Preface

This is a manual to assist parents in training and retraining their children so that the home will be happy and efficient, organized but pleasant—with parents who are satisfied with their children and children who are growing up to be respectful, responsible, resourceful, and responsive. We devote many pages to the solution of specific problems likely to arise in most families between parent and child. We also suggest ways to make the home, in general, a more harmonious place for every member of the family, whether old or young.

We are indebted to many individuals for the ideas in this book. A listing of all colleagues who have helped us understand human behavior is impossible. However, we are especially grateful to our teacher, the late Dr. Rudolf Dreikurs, who introduced us to Adlerian psychology as applied to family relationships. We wish to thank Dr. Kleona Rigney for her generous assistance and constructive criticisms. Next we wish to thank our own children, from whom we have learned a great deal in the give-and-take of family living.

Special thanks go to four counselors of the Family Education Centers of Hawaii—Marsanne Eyre, Mary Hayward, Charles Schuetz, and Sally Vernon—who read the complete manuscript and gave us invaluable suggestions.

Most of all, we are grateful to the many who have come to us for counsel. From them we have learned much while helping them to create happier homes.

RAYMOND J. CORSINI, PH.D.
GENEVIEVE PAINTER, ED.D.

Happy families are all alike; every unhappy
family is unhappy in its own way.

LEO N. TOLSTOY

I | FUNDAMENTALS OF PRACTICAL PARENTING

1 | *The Ideal Family— The Ideal Child*

When Grandmother Brown got off the airplane, her husband, Val, met her.

"How are Elinor and the kids?" he asked.

"Fine," she replied. "I had a very nice stay."

"Good," Val said, but he sounded doubtful. Only the year before, their visit with their daughter Elinor, her husband, Allan, and their three children had been a disaster.

"Val, you wouldn't believe how changed those children are. I went there expecting the worst—crying, demanding, disobedient brats. I thought Elinor would be a nervous wreck. I remembered how angry Allan was with the kids. But this time it was a pleasure to be with them. You should have come."

Val Brown looked at his wife carefully. "Is that the truth?"

His wife replied, "It's like a miracle. The children were friendly, polite, affectionate, even respectful. I asked Elinor what on earth had happened.

"She said she had gone to her doctor for ulcer symptoms and she told him how she was run ragged, chasing and fighting those kids all day long. The doctor advised her to go to a Family Education Center. There she learned how to cope. In only one month, she told me—and Allan agreed with her—fighting had practically stopped, the children didn't clutter the house anymore, Dennis wasn't dawdling, Penny no longer sucked her thumb, riding in the car wasn't a horror, Harry was doing better in school—just about *everything* had changed for the better. Then things did start to go bad again, but Elinor and Allan persisted with the program. After about three months, things got straightened out again, and now they've been going well for almost a year.

"Elinor remembers how upset you were at your last visit and how you said you'd come back when the children were all grown up. But you won't have to wait that long—you'll be happy at your next visit. We were discussing it at their family council."

"Family council?" Val asked. "What's that?"

"It's how their family operates. It's a sort of democracy in the home. They have a weekly family meeting, where they discuss things, make decisions, settle problems."

"You say Dennis doesn't dawdle anymore? How on earth did they accomplish that?"

"Oh, it was simple. They stopped waiting for him. At dinnertime, instead of having to stay at the table until he ate everything, Dennis was to serve himself, taking what he wanted. After about twenty minutes, when everyone else had finished eating, they took his plate away."

"They took his food away?"

"Yes, and it worked; he eats well now. If he wasn't ready to go someplace, they just put him in the car in his pajamas and he had to dress in the car. They call it 'logical consequences.' "

Such success stories are common in our experience. Parents *do* learn to change their ways. Children *do* learn to accommodate to new parental strategies. Families *do* become better organized, more efficient, happier.

There are, of course, many systematic ways of dealing with family relationships and problems. The system we favor was developed by Dr. Alfred Adler, an Austrian psychiatrist who started child guidance centers in Vienna in 1922, the forerunners of the Adlerian parent education centers in the United States. In the half century since 1922, hundreds of such Adlerian centers have been established, and tens of thousands of families have been counseled.

The essence of the Adlerian system of family relationships is *respect*. Parents must learn to respect themselves; they must also learn to respect their children.

WHAT IS RESPECT?

We all know the meaning of this word in its usual sense. In what sense are we using it with regard to family relations? What is disrespectful parent behavior?

In our judgment, generally, it is disrespectful for parents to:
—tell children what or how much to eat (except, of course, for poisonous substances)
—do work that the children should do for themselves
—scold children
—punish them
—reward them
—nag them
—caution them repeatedly about the same things
—clean up after them
—censor their friendships
—control their money
—permit them to dawdle
—interfere in their schoolwork
—repeat orders.

OUR IDEAL CHILD

Individual Psychology, the school of thought established by Dr. Alfred Adler, stresses human dignity and freedom. Our approach stresses consideration for both children and parents. We believe that functioning as a parent can be the most exciting and rewarding part of life. Alas, only too often parents find that their children cause them a great deal of difficulty. More than any other single factor, quarrels about children disturb marriages—more than problems about money, sex, or in-laws.

Although parents want good children, they usually do not know how to train them. Over the years, in dealing with thousands of parents, we have found that almost all of them agree that the ideal child should have what we call the four R's:

Respect
Our ideal child is considerate about the feelings of others. He treats them fairly. He does not permit others to mistreat him.

Children become respectful when treated respectfully.

Responsibility

Our ideal child contributes to the family well-being. He is helpful in the home. He does his chores without needing reminding. He participates willingly in family life and does not act like a prince who expects service.

Children become responsible by being given responsibility.

Resourcefulness

Our ideal child takes care of himself. He can entertain himself. He can meet new people and new situations. He is independent and self-reliant.

Children become resourceful if permitted to solve life's problems.

Responsiveness

Our ideal child is friendly, affectionate, and loving. He likes adults, and to be with him is a pleasure. He enjoys life. As part of the family, he receives love and reaches out for it.

Children become responsive when treated fairly with love and respect.

If children are consistently treated in respectful ways as responsible people, if they are required to use their own resources to solve their problems, and if the attitudes of the parents are friendly and loving, children will achieve the four R's. Angry, rebellious, uncooperative, hostile, or vengeful children are usually the result of a lack of parental know-how. Many parents simply don't know how to handle their jobs. They don't understand the child. They don't understand human behavior. They have incorrect concepts about discipline and training.

Respectful attitude

Disrespectful attitude

2 | *Fundamentals of Child Development*

A child inherits certain propensities, lives in a particular environment, observes what goes on about him, and interprets those observations accurately or erroneously—*in his own unique way.* He interacts with, and adapts to, members of his family. Through experience he discovers which actions succeed and which ones fail.

The family constellation

Each child has a special position within the family, and this plays a significant part in the growth of his personality. The family begins with a couple. The first child usually receives much attention—he gets much and gives little. When the second baby is born, all intrafamily relationships change. The "first" baby becomes the old one and must establish himself in a new position. The newborn is now the "baby" of the family, but this position differs from that formerly held by the child who entered the family first. And the parents now must deal with *two* children.

With each new baby the family constellation becomes bigger and more complex, with a wider range of interactions and a new position for each child. As the family constellation changes, each finds his place in his own way. An older child may strive to stay ahead of the baby, or he may give up. A second child may resent the first and may try to surpass him, or he may give up. Not all first-born children run to keep ahead of the others, and not all last children remain "babies" always in need of help. Each child tries to gain recognition in some way. If a first child does well academically, a second may cede school to the older child and may become the most charming family member. Or he may become the most ambitious child, seeking to surpass all the others.

The child's "life style" is determined by his experiences and his interpretations of them. "Who am I? What is my place?" He may conclude: "I have a place only if I am on top—or am always right —or am treated as a prince—or always please others." These responses are basic mistakes because they spring from mistaken attitudes.

Desire for competence

The baby strives to grasp a spoon. Once he has it, he is triumphant and waves the spoon in great glee. We note a similar "drive for competency" in people who work for years to receive a diploma, promotion, or pension. This drive—to become smarter, more attractive, more competent—is a basic force that pushes people into action. It is an inherent motivation, the urge to move from minus to plus.

Desire to belong

Most children also want to find a secure place within their family and within society. Children generally have a strong impulse to identify with others. This is a basic urge: to be part of a group, a community—to *belong*.

Conflict of directions

The desire for competence and the desire for belonging may pull a child in different directions at the same time. The search for competence elicits competitiveness and a desire for superiority—feelings that can corrode a sense of belonging to a group. Some children become power-seekers, wanting always to be first, to be best, to be dominant. Other children show an urgent desire to be liked by being excessively pleasing and charming. Often the domineering child makes few friends, while the child who tries always to please may become angry if his efforts go unnoticed or may behave like a "martyr" who feels misunderstood and mistreated.

Social interest

Adler called the feeling of belonging to others while at the same time feeling good about oneself *social interest.* A child with social interest recognizes that his family is devoted to him, likes him, and has confidence in him. He feels: "These are *my* people and I want to help them." At the same time he feels: "I am an O.K. person; I like myself, and I can do things for myself and for others." This child will work toward the good of the whole family. The same attitudes will later determine his role and behavior in adult society.

Parental guidance

The wise parent understands that his child operates to improve his status while at the same time he responds to the needs of others because he wishes to belong. The wise parent allows the child sufficient latitude to develop without letting him encroach upon the rights of others.

Children's goals

The parent can be a successful guide for his child's development if he understands the goals of child behavior. An encouraged child who has faith in himself and in others holds *cooperation* as a goal of behavior. But a discouraged child who feels unfairly treated, whether because of overindulgence or overrepression and punishment, refuses to cooperate. Instead of pursuing useful goals, he may seek useless ones. Dreikurs and Soltz* categorized these useless goals as:

1. Excessive *attention*—wanting to keep everyone busy with him, requesting special services, clowning, and/or being a nuisance.

2. *Power* through negativism—trying to show everyone that he will not do what he is asked.

3. *Revenge* through disobedience and other misbehavior, including delinquent behavior.

* Rudolf Dreikurs and Vicki Soltz, *Children: The Challenge* (New York: Duell, Sloan & Pearce, 1964).

4. *Inadequacy*—playing the baby, acting as though worthless, incapable, hopeless.

A child's misbehavior may result from pursuit of one or more of these four goals. Usually he is not precisely aware of what he wants to achieve. He may be misbehaving to get *attention*, or to demonstrate his *power*. Or his behavior may be a *revenge* tactic, which says in effect, "I can hurt you by not doing what you request." Or it may be a manifestation of *inadequacy*, which purports to say, "It's not my fault; I just can't stop doing it."

You can tell which goal your child is seeking by his behavior if you will examine your own feelings in reaction to it:

1. If you feel annoyed or smothered by your child's requests, his goal is probably *excessive attention*.

2. If you feel anger or resentment, his goal is likely to be *power*.

3. If you feel hurt and upset by your child's behavior, his goal may well be *revenge*.

4. If you feel helpless when confronted by your child's apparent inabilities, the goal of his behavior is quite probably a defensive, assumed inadequacy.

3 | *Democracy—Not Authoritarianism*

Many parents try to operate under an authoritarian system—"You do what I say or else!" But in today's environment the child often rebels and will do what the parents wish only under compulsion. Indeed, more and more children refuse to obey arbitrary rules regardless of the severity of punishment. This angers authoritarian parents, and sometimes a result is a "battered child syndrome," in which the child gets beaten with such harshness that he lands in the hospital.

What is required is not the assertion of authority but the establishment of mutual respect! Parents must respect children—give them freedom of action, consider their wishes, grant them independence, and no longer regard them as property. Parents must also respect themselves and require respect from their children: *Respect demands respect.*

We should deemphasize love as the primary bond between parents and children and emphasize respect. Love will be even stronger when relationships between parents and children are mutually respectful. A loving parent can damage his child through disrespectful behavior. Because of love, parents often overprotect a child and shelter him from valuable experiences. But this cannot happen when respect is the primary bond between them. Respect cannot harm.

STATEMENTS REFLECTING ATTITUDES

Authoritarian	Democratic
Stop!	Let's think about this and talk it over.
Watch yourself!	I think that's dangerous.
Because I say so!	Let's discuss it.
Come in at once.	We agreed this would be the time to come in.
Take your medicine.	Doctor says you need this medicine.
Go to bed right now!	Let's figure a good time to go to bed.
You do the chores I assigned or you get a licking.	Let's plan chores together.
Because you are fighting, go to your room.	I'm leaving. I'll come back when you kids stop fighting.
Eat what I put on your plate.	Take what you want.
Wake up right now!	Here's an alarm clock for you.
Wear what I tell you.	I feel uncomfortable when you wear that.
Take a bath; you smell!	When you smell bad, you must not stay near me.
Do your homework!	Your schoolwork is up to you.

Democracy

We suggest that parent-child relationships should catch up with our political ideals and be based on equality. We advocate that the family become, insofar as feasible, a democracy.

Does this mean that every issue has to be voted on? *No:* Voting does not work in family affairs because someone loses. Rather than majority rule, what is needed is consensus. Unanimity must be sought on all issues. Reasoning—explanation and discussion—should always be the order of the day.

Does this mean that the parent cannot say "No"? That the parent loses all authority? Again the answer is *no*. Parents *do* have responsibilities, and they *do* have authority. A parent should take a knife or a bottle of poison away from a child, who may be incompetent to judge the danger. The parent has responsibilities to laws, to the rest of his family, to his own conscience, to his financial situation—and he must respect his own rights.

The democratic system of child-rearing advocated by us has these features:

1. Equality of all members of the family, each contributing to the family in proportion to his ability.

2. An orderly way of functioning established democratically through discussions.

3. The inviolability of certain rights of the individual, such as privacy and self-determination in personal areas.

4. Straight and honest dealings between family members.

5. No forcing of one person's will upon another.

6. No harsh punishments.

7. No manipulations, such as bribes and blackmail.

8. Family relationships based on logic and reason.

9. Logical and natural consequences as a major training method (see Chapter 5).

10. Mutual respect among parents and children.

11. Parents who are friendly but at the same time firm with their children.

12. A unanimous, harmonious effort for mutual as well as individual goals.

These are attitudes and steps that we'd like you, the parent, to take:

Have confidence in children.

Some parents see children as inadequate, weak, dangerous, self-destructive—they think that unless children are constantly watched they will perish. Overfearfulness is harmful to children. The "good mother syndrome" in exaggerated form is decidedly bad.

Stop pampering.

A closely related and equally erroneous parental failing is to give children constant attention and service. Spoiling is harmful to children—it gives them an incorrect view of life and makes them dependent and demanding.

Stop overestimation.

Some parents overestimate their children, thinking that they are the smartest, the cutest, the best. Such parents often expect their children to be given preferred treatment. Such overestimation is harmful to them.

Stop oversupervision.

Some parents believe that they should always know what the child is doing—that they should hover over him, watching him constantly. Such parents monitor his friends, check his schoolwork, etc. They attempt virtually total surveillance. Needless to say, such smothering is harmful.

To see where you are at this point, check your reactions to the following:
1. To be a parent is an exciting, wonderful adventure.
2. I will do all I can to help my children grow up to be healthy, efficient, happy.
3. I respect each of my children's individuality and uniqueness.
4. I am willing to give my children as much freedom of choice and action as is consistent with their survival.
5. I will avoid doing things "for their benefit" that may result in their feeling that I am unfair.
6. I view them as my equals; but I know they are immature, and I stand ready to direct and guide them in a friendly manner.
7. I must be tolerant—after all, they are children and will act and think like children.
8. I realize that I do not own them but have only temporary custody of them.

9. I accept that I should become unnecessary to them as soon as possible so that they can go into the world on their own.

If you are in accord with those statements, all you need are some guidelines to implement the attitudes they express. You will, we hope, find these guidelines in this book.

4 | *Rewards and Punishments: A Mistake*

Many people believe the best way to train a child is to reward him when he does something they like and punish him when he does something they don't like. And it is unquestionably true that in this way they can "shape" a child's behavior. However, *rewards and punishments can have undesired side effects.* The rewarded or punished child may become dependent and fearful, rebellious and antagonistic, sneaky and untruthful, servile and unsure of himself.

As child-training devices, rewards and punishments have serious flaws. They are incompatible with human dignity. They show lack of respect. They glorify force and power. A reward is often a bribe; punishment is often revenge. They are examples of superior-inferior relationships.

The king gives his vassal a gift. A general gives a private a medal. The father gives his child a dollar. In each case a superior gives to an inferior a bounty for good behavior. The father who says, "I'll take you to the ball game if you get a haircut," is bribing his child. Mother says, "If you make your bed I'll give you a quarter." The next day the child says, "If you give me a quarter, I'll make my bed." The child thus learns to blackmail his parents.

The king demands work from a peasant; if the latter refuses, he is punished. If a private goes AWOL, the general court-martials him. If a child does not do what he is told, he gets scolded. In each case we have a superior bossing an inferior.

Frequently, punishment is meted out simply because the parent knows no other way of dealing with the child. Punishment comes in many forms: physical abuse (slapping, spanking), verbal abuse (scolding, humiliating), deprivation (being sent to bed without dinner, not being permitted to watch television), isolation (being made to stay in one's room alone for a specific period of time), grounding (not being allowed to go out with friends), etc. A brief against punishment as a child-training method could make these additional points:

1. Punishment is usually an arbitrary exercise of power by the parent, who alone decides whether, when, and how much to punish.

The parent becomes prosecutor, jury, judge, and warden. "Might is right," the child may conclude—power is what counts.

2. Punishment often is not logically related to the offense.

If we tell a child that he cannot see television because he didn't wash his hands, there is no logical relationship between the "crime" and the "punishment."

3. Punishment creates resentments.

The child may think parents are unfair because the punishment was disproportionate to the offense.

4. Punishment tends to create character defects.

The punished child will tend thereafter to try to avoid detection. He may begin to be sneaky and lie.

5. A child may lose respect for order.

If a child is punished too lightly, he may try to get away with other offenses—after all, he may reason, the penalty isn't too bad.

6. The child may try to get even.

If a child feels he has been unfairly punished, he may try to get revenge, by hurting himself or his parents, or both. The so-called Samson phenomenon of punishing both oneself and others does sometimes occur with often-punished children. They may become wild, rebellious, and delinquent.

7. The child may begin to punish also.

By punishing the child, you teach him that this is a way to treat others. He is likely to adopt punitive tactics against animals, other children, and even you, his parent.

8. Punishment has to be discontinued eventually.

When their child reaches a certain age, parents just have to give up this procedure. An attempt by a parent to punish a big child may result in a situation very ugly for both.

9. Punishment is not effective for the long-range most important objectives.

At the moment punishment may stop objectionable behavior. But if the child stops only because of fear of punishment, he is likely to refrain from undesirable behavior only while the fear remains. He is not helped to develop inner controls for good behavior. Parents should not merely try to stop particular forms of misbehavior; their primary, overriding goal should be to help the child become co-operative. The punished child often develops undesirable characteristics—lying, cheating, sneaking; he is not likely to learn to cooperate for the good of all. Punishment not only exacts a heavy toll from the child but seriously disrupts family harmony.

10. Punishment tends to become more and more severe and at the same time to become less and less a deterrent for bad behavior.

Parents who horribly mistreat their child usually do so as a result of his having ceased to fear punishment. When spanking holds no terrors for him, the parent may resort to whipping, and when this too fails to deter, may in baffled fury go to appalling lengths.

11. Punishment may actually encourage misbehavior.

Under some circumstances a child may actually misbehave *in order to obtain punishment!* And the more often, the more quickly the parent punishes, the more often the child misbehaves.

Father is looking at a newspaper. His five-year-old son tugs at his arm and demands that Father play with him. Father says "No!"

several times, but the boy keeps coming back. Finally, Father yells at him, "I swear, you're just asking for a licking!"

The child continues pulling on Father's arm and suddenly, in exasperation, Father slaps him. The child begins to screech with wild fury. Remorsefully, Father looks at his beloved five-year-old, who only wanted to play, and picks him up. "Jimmy! Quiet down. I didn't hurt you that bad. Father *loves* you. Let's play! Here is a quarter. Let's look at your comic book. I'll get on my knees and we'll play horsie."

After a while the boy's sobs slow down, his tears are dried, Father gets on his knees, and Jimmy rides on Father's back, giggling with glee.

Asking for punishment *was* worthwhile!

Here is an example of a situation that could be handled well or poorly. Ralph and Carol asked their son Chris to please go downstairs and put their name on a blackboard at the tennis club for eight A.M. He agreed, and came back stating he had done this. Ralph called friends to inform them that they have the tennis court reserved. When the four adults meet the next day to play tennis, their names are not listed for eight A.M., but for eight P.M. The parents were furious, the guests disappointed. What to do?

Father's first reaction is to give Chris a piece of his mind; Mother's reaction is the same, although she is willing to concede he meant well, but Father believes this is another example of Chris's playing "dumb" and sabotaging his parents.

Were the parents to vent their feelings against Chris, this would be punishment, and would make him feel more inadequate, more fearful, and less inclined to do things for them. But what should be done in such situations?

Almost anything but punishment is preferable. Saying nothing would be one solution. Telling him in a humorous way what happened would be another way to handle this. What counts is that the child should not feel humiliated, alienated or hostile. Everyone can make a mistake. The child meant well. To punish him in any manner will simply drive him underground, make him resentful, less cooperative.

Adlerians see problems—and this is an example of a problem—as opportunities. Ralph and Carol can use this situation to actually strengthen relationships—if they are wise enough to deal with it sensibly.

Neither rewards nor punishments are effective training methods for today's children. The best way for a parent to correct misbehavior and yet maintain good relations is the method called *logical and natural consequences,* discussed in the next chapter.

5 | *Natural and Logical Consequences*

What should we do if we don't punish or reward? Parents should always try first to obtain voluntary cooperation from their children by encouragement, being cooperative themselves, and by using democratic procedures in the home. If these fail, parents should fall back on the method widely known as *natural and logical consequences*.

This method is in accord with reality and helps to prepare the child for the ways in which nature and society are going to react to his behavior.

Natural consequences

A woman who had been attending one of our child guidance centers summarized natural consequences thus: "When a chlld does something wrong, you don't hit or scold him; you do nothing. You let the situation get worse and worse until the child becomes uncomfortable or sees for himself that the situation has become ridiculous. Finally, he makes changes on his own." She was quite right: *The essence of natural consequences is to let the child learn from experience.*

A mother complains that her son is a poor eater and that she has to nag to get him to eat. We regard constant nagging as punishment. We advise her to employ natural consequences, that is, to stop her nagging and to allow him to learn by experience.

The following morning, her son rushes out to play without having eaten his breakfast. Several hours later, he is famished. He is experiencing the natural consequences of not having eaten breakfast. *She does not give him food until lunchtime.*

A toddler is intrigued with the shiny toaster and wants to handle it while Mother is using it. Mother says, "Don't touch it. It's hot." But the young master insists and gets burned. Instead of scolding or preaching, Mother merely puts ointment on the burn. He has experienced the natural consequences of his behavior.

A child insists on wearing a particularly odd article of clothing. Mother says nothing and does not interfere. He goes out wearing the item, but he returns within a few minutes and removes it because other children laughed at him.

A child straps on his skates incorrectly. Father points out the error, but the son thinks he knows better. When he stands up, his skates fall off.

A child wants to see a late television movie. Mother reminds him that he must get up early for school and won't get enough sleep. He says he will. Mother lets him stay up. In the morning he feels groggy and tired.

A boy teases his companion until the other boy hits him and leaves him.

A child refuses to clean his desk. His parents say nothing. Eventually, the top of his desk is completely littered, and he does his homework on his bed. This is uncomfortable, and he cleans off his desk so he can use it.

In relying upon natural consequences, parents will discover that nature is their best ally. A child who doesn't eat gets hungry; one who plays too hard gets tired; one who forgets to take money for a school lunch goes without; one who cheats at games finds himself without playmates; one who neglects his homework discovers that his teachers call him to account.

Parents must, of course, be alert to nullify any possibility of serious harm to the child. Certainly he cannot be permitted to fall out of a window or to eat poisonous substances. Natural consequences must be used *with discretion.*

Parents have an obligation to inform this child *once* of the natural consequences of any specific behavior. If they keep reminding him, they are either giving him unwarranted service or punishing him by nagging. One such warning in a lifetime is usually enough.

Parents should not feel that they are cruel when, within reasonable limits, they allow their child to experience the natural but unpleasant consequences of his behavior. Parents should not intervene between him and reality except in emergencies. What more can a parent do for a child than to help him learn the consequences he must face when he violates the laws of nature or society? In our tender youth, we came near a swarm of bees. "Don't go near them," Father warned. "They can sting!" And so we learned by sad experience a lesson that after forty years remains: bees do sting!

Logical consequences

Natural consequences alone are not sufficient to train a child. In many cases parents must do something more. The course of action we recommend is called *logical consequences.* It is more effective than punishment but has none of punishment's drawbacks. It requires an understanding, expressed (preferable) or implied, between a parent and the child as to what is expected from the child and what is to happen if the child does not perform as expected or misbehaves. What happens then must be a logical consequence to the child's conduct.

Father tells his child that he will take him to the movies if ready by three o'clock. The child asks at four o'clock to be taken to the movies. Father simply says, "You knew you were to be ready by three. Now it's four. I'm sorry. I will not take you now."

Little Bobby is whooping and hollering in the living room where Father and Mother are reading. Father says, "If you can't be quiet, go to your room." Father now has an understanding with Bobby: *If you are quiet, you may remain; if not, you must go.* Bobby continues making noise and Father says firmly but without anger, "Go to your room. Come back when you can behave yourself."

The child is always given a choice and parents must not show anger. If the parent is angry or doesn't offer a choice, the technique is *not a consequence but is punishment, and it won't work.* The following parental statements illustrate the techniques of logical consequences:

"If you don't behave yourself at the restaurant, I will take you home."

"Unless you agree to act properly at the supermarket, I will not take you there."

"If you lose your money, I will not give you any more."

"If you break the window playing ball, you'll have to pay for a replacement."

"If you don't eat at lunchtime, you cannot eat until supper."

When the understanding is clear and consistently followed, the child cannot feel that his parent is being unfair to him and so he harbors no resentment.

Ignoring or withdrawing as a logical consequence.

Some parents frequently find themselves arguing with a child with the hope of persuading him to stop unwanted behavior. They do not realize that ignoring or withdrawing from a child's misbehavior is a better way to teach than talking.

Let us suppose that you are reading a newspaper, like the father in the example given earlier, and that your child perists in begging you to play with him. You feel tired, and this is not his time for playing with you. You have already told him so, but he continues to whine. *You leave the room and go somewhere else to finish reading your paper. You withdraw from his behavior.* Or suppose you are having breakfast and the children are noisy. *You pick up your toast and cup of coffee and finish your breakfast in the living room. You withdraw.*

When we advise parents to withdraw from a child's tyrannical behavior, they often try to equate such withdrawal with defeat, with running away from a situation. They are wrong. Withdrawal here simply means going from a spot where there is trouble to one where there is none. It gives this message: "When I don't like *what you do*, I go away from you." When we use withdrawal as a training technique, we must be careful to indicate that we are not fleeing from the individual but rather from his *behavior.*

Leaving the child can be effective means of discouraging annoying behavior no matter what his goal may be. If he is acting silly to get attention, if he is trying to initiate an argument to show his power, if he is pretending disability in order to get you to do things for him, if he is having a temper tantrum, often all you need do is ignore him or withdraw from him. In this simple way you terminate the child's useless behavior and teach him that it will not work!

Parents often wonder why withdrawal is so effective. The child's behavior is purposive. If he wants to get you involved against your will and you resort to punishment, you *have* become involved. But if you vanish, you do not become involved, and you frustrate the child's attempt to force his goal-oriented behavior on you.

The bathroom technique as a logical consequence.

After a season of family counseling, we recently asked the assembled mothers what had impressed them most. One young mother enthusiastically stated: "The bathroom technique! It's the answer I've been seeking for years."

Suggested by Dr. Rudolf Dreikurs, the bathroom technique is almost absurdly simple: when children press you with their demands, withdraw to the one room in every household in which a person can barricade himself—the bathroom! We recommend this technique to mothers harrassed by demanding younger children. The mother who wants to escape the tyranny of her child's demands enters the bathroom and locks the door. While there, she does not respond in any way to the child—even if he whines, cries, screams, or hits the door. If he continues, she turns on the radio, and if he still persists, she takes a bath! She concentrates on composing herself, but at the same time she is training her child. When all is calm, she comes out with a smile. But if the child reasserts his demands or exhibits other undesired behavior, back she goes to the bathroom!

If there is only one bathroom in the house, the clever child may suddenly scream, "Wee-wee!" What should Mother do now? *She should remain in the bathroom.* The child is being trained. The message that Mother is getting across is that she will no longer take any nonsense. If the enraged child begins to hammer on the door or to break furniture, Mother should still stay in the bathroom! The event may have a powerful effect on the child; it may be for him a crisis that profoundly changes his perception of Mother. If Mother is foolish enough to come out when the child threatens, she loses a very effective training device. Once she has entered the bathroom, she should leave only when she is ready, not when the child wants her to. She should not come out until she is calm and relaxed. The most helpful thing for her to think about her stay inside is that her child is being taught to improve his behavior.

The waking technique as a logical consequence.

Although we are against punishment, our methods are not necessarily passive. We use what *works*. The waking technique is a valuable but unpleasant tactic based on logical consequences. The understanding involved may be summarized as follows: The child promises to perform an agreed-upon task and his parents promise not to nag him about it; however, the child agrees that the parents can remind him *at any time, day or night* if he forgets to do as he promised.

Ken had the chore of taking out the garbage. Mother wanted him to do this before he went to bed, since she didn't want garbage in the house overnight. Ken agreed, but kept "forgetting." Mother sometimes had to remind him two or three times an evening. And sometimes both he and Mother forgot and the garbage remained overnight. This situation had been going on for more than a year, with periodic bouts of scolding.

Mother was advised to employ the waking technique. She told Ken, "From now on, is it all right for me to remind you to empty the garbage at any time, day or night?" Ken agreed. That night, Mother noticed that Ken went to bed without having emptied the garbage. As soon as she heard him get into bed, she knocked on his door and reminded him of his chore. He got up and emptied the garbage. The next night he again forgot. At ten, when he was fast asleep, Mother knocked on his door. She had to remind him several times before he understood what was wanted of him. He then emptied the garbage. The next night he remembered. The night after that he forgot and Mother awakened him again. Within ten days the garbage problem had been completely solved. He never forgot again.

Our experience with the waking technique is that typically a child requires to be awakened three or four times to fix permanently in his memory the chore he is supposed to do.

To prevent this from being punishment, the child must freely agree to being reminded at night. Rarely have we found a child who will not agree. And we have known children who asked that just this be done—to help them to learn to remember!

To be reminded after he has fallen asleep is an unpleasant but logical consequence. If a parent does undertake this technique, he must use it consistently. If the child is awakened and goes back to sleep without doing what he is supposed to do, then he must be reawakened, gently but firmly, usually by knocking on the door at fifteen-minute intervals, until he does it.

In the subsequent part of our book in which we discuss specific problems, we shall suggest a wide variety of logical consequences. The two we have just discussed (moving away from the child when he misbehaves and reminding him of what he is supposed to do but at an inconvenient time) are very general ones.

We have never yet been confronted with any situation that calls for a child's punishment. All misbehavior by children can be handled best by the method of natural and logical consequences. If parents will just begin to think logically rather than punitively, they will start to treat their children with respect and will be on the way to a happier family life.

6 | *Encouraging the Child*

Encouragement is the nourishment of the soul just as food is the nourishment of the body. Any uncooperative child is likely to be a discouraged one.

PITFALLS OF DISCOURAGEMENT

A discouraged person is usually convinced that he is not as adequate as others; he often gives up without even trying.

Unwittingly, parents frequently discourage this child. Indeed, in their very attempts to encourage him, they often achieve just the opposite result.

Discouraging statements made prior to behavior

Don't get dirty.
Watch yourself.
You aren't old enough.
Be careful.
Let me do it for you.
Let me show you how.
I know you can't do it.
If younger children can do it, so can you.
Look at how well your cousin does it.

Discouraging statements made after behavior

> No, that's not right.
> I should not have trusted you.
> You could have done better.
> You should have watched me.
> I've told you a thousand times.
> When will you become responsible?
> You did it again.
> Oh, when will you learn?
> I am so ashamed of you.
> Haven't you any self-respect?
> I'll tell your father when he gets home.
> If you'd only listen to me.
> If only you weren't so lazy.
> You'll be sorry when I'm dead.

Normal parents who love their child frequently talk this way. They want their remarks to make him try harder. And in the immediate situation this may happen: to get his parents' approval, the child may make a special effort. However, negative parental remarks do not work in the long run. If he gets a steady diet of such discouraging remarks, the child eventually feels: What's the use? I can't do things. I can't win. I can never satisfy them. Everyone does better than I do. *I won't try anymore.* He usually feels this way unconsciously—without awareness.

ENCOURAGEMENT

Encouragement implies your faith in the child—communicates your belief in his strength and ability.

Parents easily see their child's weak points; they should look hard to find his strong points. No matter how trivial those may seem, it is wise to let him know they are appreciated. Sometimes we hear a parent say something such as this: "I can't see anything good about Billy; he irritates me all the time." It is difficult for a parent, when irritated, to see the child's good qualities. At such a time, it is important for the parent to rise above the irritation and to say positive rather than negative things to the child. Always there is at least some small point upon which the parent can focus an encouraging remark. "You made a good try at getting your newspapers delivered on time," one mother said to her son, whom she had usually criticized for late deliveries on his paper route. The boy was faster the next day.

The dangers of praise

Praise may or may not be encouraging. Lavish praise usually seems insincere. The child may feel he is not worthy of it. Praise may actually discourage a child if he fears that next time he may not be able to live up to it.

One praises when a job is well done. However, when a child does poorly, he needs encouragement much more than when he does well.

HOW TO DISTINGUISH BETWEEN PRAISE AND ENCOURAGEMENT

1. Praise is given to the *doer:* "You are a good boy for drawing such a nice picture for me."

1. Encouragement is given for the *deed:* "That is a pretty picture" or "I'm sure you enjoyed drawing your picture."

2. Praise is given for work well done: What good grades you have brought home!"

2. Encouragement is also given when work is done poorly: "So what—we all make mistakes; I'm sure you'll do better next time."

3. Praise implies a demand for continued high performance.

3. Encouragement makes no demands.

4. Praise often seems phony.

4. Encouragement is sincere.

5. Praise may not increase self-esteem.

5. Encouragement fosters self-esteem.

How to encourage your child

1. Build on his strong points.

Look for good things, including his efforts.

2. Do not emphasize his liabilities.

Do not criticize, nag, or complain about what he should have done.

3. Show your appreciation.

"I do enjoy hearing the songs you sing." "I appreciate your setting the table and making the salad; it makes my dinner preparation so much easier."

4. Be friendly.

A friend shares and listens: "You seem troubled; want to talk?" "I met Jerry's mother at the grocery today." Just sitting nearby is friendly.

5. Show your affection.

A kiss, a hug, or an arm around the shoulder causes the child to feel that you like him.

6. Suggest small steps in doing a task.

The entire job may seem too much. Give small portions of food to a finicky eater; when he finds himself asking for seconds, he'll be encouraged.

7. Spend time in play with the child.

Through play you can build a good relationship.

8. Use humor.

A wiggled nose, a wink, a pun, or a laugh at oneself can warm the relationship. Always laugh *with* the child, never at him.

9. Notice an attempt to do a job.

Recognize his effort even if the job is not well done.

10. Become fully aware of the interaction between yourself and your child.

The child will at times provoke your anger by testing you to the limits of your endurance. At such times it is best not to show anger but just to walk away and stay away until you cool off. When both are calm, you may tell him that such behavior angers you.

11. Discipline the child in silence.

Angry words are extremely discouraging. After disciplining, resume talking or you will appear unfriendly.

12. Mind your own business.

Learn to depend upon the method called natural consequences. Allow the child to solve his own problems. Don't be on his back at all times; give him the widest latitude possible in attending to his concerns and interests.

13. Don't use rewards or punishment.

They do not encourage.

14. Accept the child as he is.

The more emphatically you do so, the more emphatically you tell him "I like you."

15. Be understanding.

Try to see the world from the child's point of view. And don't forget that you yourself can sometimes be wrong.

16. Have faith in your child.

Who knows what your child may become? The kid who isn't doing his homework, who gets into your things, who does not want to go to bed on time, who messes up his room, who fights with his brothers and sisters—who knows but what he may become a fine success someday. Author? Minister? Doctor? United States senator? President?

17. Be an optimistic person yourself.

Children often pick up the attitudes of their parents. If you are gloomy and dissatisfied, your child may adopt your outlook. Instead of thinking: It won't work, think: Maybe it will work.

7 | *General Rules for Child Training*

In this chapter we give parents general rules and principles for implementing the specific recommendations we make in the chapters that follow. Here we are concerned with HOW the parent acts. In the rest of the book we are concerned primarily with WHAT the parent does. Success depends just as much on *how* you deal with children as *what* you do.

Father and mother should read this chapter carefully and come to complete agreement about its contents. They might well read this chapter aloud, stopping to discuss each point.

FOUR FUNDAMENTAL RULES FOR DISCIPLINING A CHILD

1. **Understand** exactly what you are supposed to do. Do not tackle a problem until you really grasp the *how* and the *why* of the advice.

2. **Inform** the child, explaining clearly what you intend to do about the problem in question. Answer all his questions.

3. **Act.** Silence is necessary during the disciplining. Warnings, reminders, discussions, threats about the problem are unwise.

4. Be consistent during the disciplining. Avoid variations and exceptions. Do not let others sway you. Do not feel sorry for the child; pity will not help to train him.

These four rules are applicable to practically every problem in nonpunitive child discipline. So, without yelling, nagging, preaching, punishing, or threatening, do exactly what you have told the child you will do, and do it consistently. Any variation is likely to necessitate a lengthening of the disciplining and may even make the training procedure fail!

Never start to discipline the child unless you are prepared to stick to the recommended procedure. You should show no anger when you explain what you are going to do or when you are doing it. The child may return your anger, and you will probably fail to effect the change you desire.

GENERAL PRINCIPLES

There can, of course, be no substitute for parental common sense. The following principles are not a substitute for sound judgment, but they should be helpful if kept in mind:
— When you don't know what to do, do nothing.
— Treat the child with the respect that you expect from him.
— Don't do things routinely for a child that he can do for himself.
— Learn to mind your own business.
— In training a child, *act* rather than talk.

WHEN PARENTS DISAGREE

"My spouse won't cooperate!"

We often hear this complaint. Most frequently the complainant is a woman who informs us that her husband is sure that he knows all the answers for family problems and that if only she will listen to him everything will be fine. Sometimes a male client informs us that his wife believes love is enough and that if he would only stop interfering things would straighten out.

WHAT TO DO IF YOUR MATE WILL NOT GO ALONG WITH YOU

Even if your spouse does not agree with the methods we advocate, he or she may not object to your following them. If they work, your spouse will see the success you are having and is likely to adopt an approach similar to yours.

After learning our ways of operating, Milly informed her husband. He pooh-poohed them but told her that she could deal with the children in those crazy ways if she wanted to. The major problem was the children's fighting. Milly began to use our methods systematically. Gradually the children stopped their fighting when Mother was around. When Father was around, they continued fighting. Eventually Father noticed the difference. He too began to use the methods Mother was using; and, sure enough, the children stopped their bickering in his presence.

If the parents are not in a power contest with each other, if each will give the other freedom to do what the other thinks best, the family problem becomes a kind of experiment—and the better method will surface.

It is better, of course, for both parents to take the same approach from the beginning. We suggest that parents read this book together, discuss its suggestions, get to understand the Adlerian theory and methods of family relationships, and then see if they can find areas of agreement so that they can as nearly as possible present a common front.

If this cannot be done but if one parent will at least permit the other to handle the children by our methods without any interference, progress will occur, though not as rapidly. But if the different approach causes dissension and there is a power contest between the parents that cannot be resolved peacefully, they should seek other ways to achieve family harmony. Such families need more help than a book can provide. A family counselor may be necessary.

UNEXPECTED BENEFITS

You may be wonderfully surprised to find that when you solve one problem, some other problems have automatically been solved too. When, for instance, you help your child learn to get himself up in the morning or to keep himself clean, you are taking him and yourself into a new and better way of life where respect and reason rule. As this new regime takes over, the old negative games involving you and your children—senseless bickerings, punishments, harrassments, and conflicts—will disappear. New and better family relationships will result. The home will become harmonious and orderly, with children who are cooperative and parents who are satisfied because they are successfully training their children for respect, responsibility, resourcefulness, and responsiveness.

IMPORTANT NOTICE

This is a do-it-yourself manual. Please pay special attention to the following points before going on to the next section, in which we deal with many specific problems involving children in routine family life.

VALIDITY AND PRACTICALITY

Every suggestion we make has been tested and found practical and effective over and over again in many, many families in actual life.

CONSISTENCY

For successful child-training, consistency is vital. If you decide to use our techniques, give them a chance to work: follow them all the way through, with firm, undeviating, absolute consistency.

STARTING

Do not start any procedure we recommend until you understand the theory and principles on which it is based.

COMMUNICATION

Trickery has no place in our system. You can let the children know exactly what you are reading; indeed, you should make this book available to them if it may interest them. You should tell them your objectives in training them. You should also tell them what you intend to do.

ATTITUDE

You must be firm and friendly at the same time. You respect your children and control your own temper—no nagging, no punishments, no violence!

FAILURE

If, using our methods, you fail in one problem, you should *not* tackle another one. Our methods have worked for thousands of families. If you really understood our theory, faithfully followed our instructions, and yet failed, our suggestion is that you drop this book and find a qualified family counselor.

FOLLOW THROUGH

If you do solve a problem, don't think it is settled for good. That problem is likely to recur, since children often "test" parents. We call that "the second offensive." Don't be dismayed. All is not lost. Use exactly the same tactics that worked the first time—in silence, of course (you do not have to explain again). The technique will work anew! Sometimes there may be a third occurrence—again, use the same techniques. A fourth offensive is very rare, practically unheard of.

II | PROBLEMS OF ROUTINE LIVING

We have already presented a considerable amount of material intended to help you understand the general approach to child-rearing that we recommend. Now you are ready to begin the process of actually retraining your children.

In this section, "Problems of Routine Living," we discuss six common problems: (1) getting up, (2) getting dressed, (3) eating, (4) cleanliness, (5) home-school relationships, and (6) bedtime.

So common are these problems that some parents think that every family must have them. It actually surprises some parents, for example, that bedtime need not be difficult, and that there are families where there never is an argument about eating or dressing. What a shame that so many families are never free from tension because of constant conflict in these everyday situations!

Besides their being so prevalent, why is the solving of these six problems so important? First, if you can solve any one of them, you can solve every other! Second, if you solve one, other problems may solve themselves. Third, success in handling one of these will give you self-confidence as a parent.

A final preliminary word: Pick only one problem of routine living, and work on this alone. When it is solved, and only then, begin on a second problem. Good luck!

8 | *Getting Up*

THE PROBLEM

"Did you call Harry and Ellen?" Father asked.

"Twice already," Mother replied testily as she turned over a pancake.

"It's seven-thirty. You'd better go wake them. I have to leave by eight. If they want to ride with me, they'd better get up."

"Please, *you* do it. I have my hands full. You'd think a boy of eleven and a girl of eight would be able to get up by themselves. Kids are just so spoiled nowadays!"

Father got up and climbed the stairs. He knocked at Harry's door and then opened it. The boy was sleeping, as usual face down. Father shook Harry, who opened his eyes slowly as he turned around.

"What time?" he asked sleepily.

"Almost a quarter to eight. You have to hurry." While Harry was rubbing his eyes, Father rushed to Ellen's room to repeat the same performance. He then went down to the kitchen.

"Every day we go through the same damn routine. This morning I'm leaving at 8 A.M., rain or shine, kids or no kids."

"But they can't leave without a good hot breakfast," Mother said, "and they can't walk to school today. It looks like rain."

Father sighed deeply. "I just don't know. When I was a kid, I used to walk a mile and a quarter to school. *Half* a mile is too much for *these* kids. One of these days I'll lose my job on account of being late so often."

Instead of answering, Mother went to the foot of the stairs and in a shrill voice yelled, "Hurry up, you kids! Breakfast is ready."

She then sat down to finish her breakfast with her husband, commenting grimly, "I wish I knew how some families manage to get their kids up without so much trouble every morning."

DISCUSSION

In many families such morning difficulties occur almost every day. Fathers and mothers are tense and upset, having called their children a number of times, knocked on doors, pleaded with them to get ready, helped them to dress, argued with them that it really is time to get up, and so on. Some parents give children a great deal of service and are almost angelic in their servitude; other parents get angry and even violent. But still other parents just do not have this trouble at all. Their kids get up on their own, take care of themselves, and leave the house without difficulty.

What is the secret? Is it a matter of temperament or physiology? Is it that the children do not get enough sleep, having worked too late on homework or watched television too long? Actually, it is none of these.

Children will learn to get up on time and take care of themselves if they must face the natural consequences of being late. This means that parents must realize that getting up is the child's business—and that they must keep out of the whole matter. The child, not his parents, must experience the consequences of being late.

SOLUTION

We suggest the following:
1. If you think your child is old enough to use an alarm clock (usually children at five are old enough), get one and teach him how to set it and how to turn it off.
2. If you prefer not to use an alarm, tell your child you will call him only one time in the morning.

3. Discuss with him the best time to be awakened, your object being to help him set an awakening time that will allow him just enough time to do his morning routine, dress, get breakfast, and take off for school.

4. If children sleep in separate rooms, you may want a separate alarm (or a separate call) for each room.

5. From then on, just keep out of the way. Say nothing more about getting up and see what happens, allowing the children to experience the natural consequences of oversleeping.

APPLICATION TO HARRY AND ELLEN'S PROBLEM

The parents had a discussion with their children.

"From now on, getting up in the morning will be *your* problem. Your mother and I will no longer assume responsibility for it," Father said.

"But we may be late for school," Harry objected.

Father's answer surprised him: "Then you'll just have to take that up with your teachers."

Ellen spoke with an air of adult concern: "But if I get up late, I won't have time to have a hot, nourishing breakfast and I may get a vitamin deficiency."

Mother's reply shook her a bit: "That's too bad. I do want us all to be healthy, but if you want your breakfast, you'll have to get up on time."

"You won't wake us up?" asked Harry. "You said I'm such a heavy sleeper. How will I know when to get up?"

Father answered, "We'll give each of you an alarm clock and show you how to set it. If you oversleep, you'll just have to explain things to your teachers. Furthermore, from now on I am leaving at exactly eight o'clock in the morning. If you're ready, then I'll be happy to give you a ride. But if you're not ready, I'll go without you."

"How will we get there?" Ellen asked, apparently rather intrigued. "What if we miss a ride with you and it's raining?"

Smiling, Mother said, "Then you'll go with a raincoat, an umbrella, and rubbers."

The parents put this procedure into effect. The first two days, the children got up with their alarm clocks, but on the third day, Harry overslept. He was not awakened by his alarm clock because he had failed to set it. Father went to school with Ellen. When Harry awoke, he was already late for school. Mother refused to let him stay home. He took off for school and got there three-quarters of an hour late.

At school his teacher asked him why he was late. When he said he had overslept, she told him he would have to stay after school for three-quarters of an hour. That night he was careful to set his alarm.

Several days later, Ellen came flying down from her room just as Father was about to start the car.

"Just a minute, Daddy. Please wait till I eat my breakfast. Please."

Father looked out of the car window and said, "I'll wait exactly one minute. I am leaving at eight."

Ellen dashed back into the house. While she was still gulping her breakfast, Father started the car and drove off. She ran out of the house, but Father had left at exactly eight o'clock. She wiped her mouth and began to walk to school. Her mother looked on in silence, realizing that Ellen was learning the hard way, through experiencing the consequences of her behavior: if she overslept, she would have to walk.

Within two weeks both children were arising promptly at the sound of their alarm clocks and were ready to leave the house at eight sharp. Even Harry, who had merited his reputation of being a "heavy sleeper," seemed transformed. The parents were no longer in the service of their children as human alarm clocks.

FURTHER EXAMPLES

The Pryor family also faced morning battles. The parents purchased an alarm clock for each child, but the kids did not use them. The parents said absolutely nothing about the matter. The children were late for school every day for a week. Eventually, the school counselor called. The conversation went as follows:

"Mrs. Pryor, are you aware that both Gail and Eve have been late every morning this week?"

"Yes, I am."

"Don't you think that you can do something about it? Why don't you get them out of bed earlier?"

"Mrs. Locke, I think that the solution should be at your end. What are *you* going to do about it?"

"Don't you think it is *your* responsibility to get your children up on time?"

"No, I don't. I think that the responsibility is the *child's*. And I think that if the school is unhappy about their lateness, the school should handle the problem."

"We have warned them several times. They just keep coming in late. We don't know what to do."

"My suggestion is that you require them to make up the time after school or to suspend them. Let them experience the consequences of their behavior."

"Aren't you interested in your children's coming to school on time?"

"Interested? Of course I am. But I think it's the child's problem, and that the issue is between her and the school."

"You have an unusual attitude, Mrs. Pryor."

"Perhaps it is different from the attitudes of most mothers, but I believe getting to school on time is the responsibility of the child and not of his parents. I believe a tardy child inconveniences his teacher and breaks a school regulation; therefore the school should confront him with his behavior and require him to face the consequences. For years I have nagged the girls without changing their behavior. I now think that you, in the school, should crack down."

"Perhaps you are right. I'll call them in and have a discussion with them."

As the days passed, Mrs. Pryor noticed that the children were getting up earlier and leaving home in time to get to school at the proper time. She said nothing about it, being wise enough to know that when children do what they are supposed to do, parents should not make a comment of any kind.

Mornings were not the happiest time of the day at the Kosak household. After talking with a family counselor, the parents held a family council with their children.

"We think you kids are old enough to get up by yourselves," Mother told Harold, Linda, and Birdie. "I am going to get you an alarm clock to keep in your room. I'll show you how to use it. What do you think of that?"

The kids were excited.

Nine-year-old Harold, the oldest, said "Can I set it?"

Mother smiled. "It will belong to all of you. What time do you think you ought to get up?"

Linda shouted, "Six o'clock!"

"That's too early," Birdie, the youngest, age six, yelled. "Seven o'clock, when Mama wakes us."

"I won't be waking you anymore," Mother said. "The alarm clock will do it, but you will all have to decide on the right time to set it."

At first the alarm was set to ring at six. The kids didn't have to leave until eight. After a week, it was set at six-thirty. Then, after several days, it was set by agreement at seven and finally, after several more days, at seven-thirty.

Thus by trial and error the children arrived at the time that was best for everyone. They were able to work this out on their own because Mother and Father did not interfere.

Eight-year-old Barry and ten-year-old Ron were given an alarm clock to share after Mother read the suggestion in a book. Without her knowing it, Ron would get up at the ring of the clock but Barry would stay in bed until Ron shook him. Mother found out when she walked by their room one morning.

She said, "Ron, you shouldn't shake your brother; he's supposed to get up by himself when he hears the alarm."

"Aw, he'll just sleep all day; he can't hear it, Mom."

Mother explained, "But if you keep this up, he'll never learn to respond to the alarm."

"He'll be late for school."

"That's the way he'll learn. Will you help him grow up?"

"O.K., but I don't think it will work."

That evening Mother told Barry that Ron had agreed with her that Barry was old enough to be responsible for his own awakening and that Ron would no longer shake him if he did not hear the clock. Barry warned them that he would not hear the alarm because he was such a sound sleeper. Neither Mother nor Ron said more.

Barry was late for school two mornings in a row, and his teacher asked him in front of the other children to give the reason for his tardiness. Barry heard the alarm the third morning and thereafter.

The Boel family had a problem in getting up that was somewhat different, since both parents had to leave their house at 8 A.M. to get to work by 9. En route they would drop off their child at school, which started at 8:30. The family routine in the morning was ridiculous, with many reminders and much nagging.

The counselor made a suggestion to the parents: call Elmer at 7:40, which was about the time he usually got up; then leave at 8 A.M., taking him along whether he was dressed or not, whether he had eaten breakfast or not. The parents were told to keep a set of clothes in the car, so Elmer could dress as they took him to school.

The parents didn't like this suggestion too well but nevertheless decided to try it. They had a talk with Elmer, who didn't like the idea either. However, the plan was put into effect, and the first morning it worked well—Elmer was ready at eight. But the next day, after Mother called Elmer, he answered sleepily, "I'm getting up," and then went back to sleep. At five to eight he was awakened by his father, who said, "We are leaving with you in five minutes." Five minutes later, unwashed, unfed, but dressed, Elmer was in the car.

A week later, Elmer again did not get up when he was awakened and at eight o'clock was still asleep. Mother awoke him and carried him to the car; and all three took off, with Elmer, unfed, in his pajamas. En route, Elmer dressed himself.

In the succeeding year there were perhaps two slip-ups, but the pattern was established: his parents knocked on his door at seven-forty, he sprang up, and was completely ready to go in twenty minutes, dressed, washed, and fed. The nonsense that all three had suffered so long was over.

A simple solution worked beautifully in a family where the mother was a worrier. She had slipped into a morning routine in which she called and called her three kids, became involved in their dressing, checked whether they had enough lunch money, supervised their eating, made sure they had their schoolbooks, etc. When the children finally left for school, she had been working for almost two hours, and was exhausted. The solution was elegantly simple: she just wasn't to get out of bed until eight-thirty—doctor's orders!

Mother fought the counselor's suggestion, but it made good sense to the father—and reluctantly she agreed. Within two weeks the kids had worked out a routine in which, on their own, they got up, dressed, prepared and ate breakfast, and managed to get to school on time, with their lunch money and schoolbooks. True, before they accepted the fact that Mother meant it, they did a lot of crying and complaining. But after all, it was doctor's orders—strict orders—for her not to be out of bed before eight-thirty.

We suggest this version of a parental strike in hard-core cases, especially with older kids, that is to say, those over ten.

S U M M A R Y

It is important for children to be responsible for their own behavior. Parents agree on this point in theory but often find it difficult to train their children to become responsible because they continue to give them unnecessary service and to overprotect them. Even a nursery school child can learn to set an alarm clock, listen for it, and get up without help from parents. This is one of the simplest ways to teach responsible behavior at a very early age.

Caution: You must have and show faith in the child's ability to heed the alarm; and you must not feel sorry for him should he experience the natural consequences of being late. That is the best way to learn—through experience.

9 | *Dressing*

Mrs. Hayward shook her head as she watched Kevin, her four-year-old, attempt to get into his undershorts. First he put one leg in, and then he tried to put the other leg in the same hole. Both feet in, he then tried to pull the shorts up, but fell over. Mother released him and patiently said, "Try again." This time he did get each leg in separately, but when he pulled them up, the pants were on backward. He took them off and refused to try again. "When will you ever learn?" Mother asked as she began to dress him.

DISCUSSION

Dressing can be a major problem. In many homes, children expect parents to dress them, refuse to learn, can't find the right clothes, and thus are late for school.

A child should become independent as soon as possible. Parents should not do for a child what he can do for himself. Many children like to keep parents occupied by expecting or even demanding service. Our general training procedure is simply to withdraw from giving undue service to a child so that he will learn to take care of himself. He probably will make many mistakes—but he will learn from them. A problem can be an opportunity for learning.

49

SOLUTION APPLIED TO KEVIN

Mrs. Hayward, after being counseled, talked with her husband, who agreed to the suggested solution: simply to refuse to dress Kevin. The next day, he came into their bedroom in his pajamas and asked to be dressed. "Sorry, Kevin," Mother said. "From now on you have to dress yourself." He immediately indulged in a temper tantrum. Father went to the kitchen. Mother ran to the bathroom and locked herself in while Kevin pounded on the door. She turned on the radio. His pounding and screaming continued. She began to fill the tub full force, put in crystals for a bubble bath, and prepared for a long soaking (see page 26). Eventually, Kevin stopped his pounding and screaming. When Mother finally finished her bath and came out, Kevin was naked. And so he remained for two days! Father would not dress him, Mother would not dress him. Whenever a visitor showed up, Kevin hid, coming out after the visitor left.

On the third day of his nakedness, Mother, upset by his constant whining and complaining, crossed the yard to her neighbor's to get away. This was the first time Kevin had ever been left alone. "I wonder," she said to the sympathetic neighbor, "whether he can really dress himself? I used to think that at least he was trying hard. But when the counselor heard that Kevin always put on his shorts backward, he said Kevin must know how to put them on properly; otherwise he would manage to get them right about fifty percent of the time!"

At that point they heard a knock on the side door. The neighbor opened the door and there stood Kevin, completely dressed.

FURTHER EXAMPLES

Mike, ten, had been told "a million times" to put his clothes in the hamper when they were dirty, but Mother kept looking in his room and picking up things, putting them in the hamper herself on the day she did laundry. Finally, she decided that she would do no more picking up and from now on would wash for him only what he put in the hamper—and so informed Mike. This information went in one ear and out the other. And Mike's shirts, shorts, socks, and pants remained on the floor of his room.

"Ma, I got nothing to wear," he said one Monday morning, coming to her in the kitchen, still wearing his pajamas.

"You have lots of things to wear."

"Nothing clean," he said patiently.

"Well, wear something dirty," she replied.

"Everything is too dirty to wear," he told her.

"Why don't you wear some of my clothes?" Father said. (Father weighed about two hunded pounds.)

"Too big for me," Mike answered.

"I'm sorry," said Mother.

"I'm sorry too," said Father.

"What should I do?" Mike asked.

"Search me," said Father.

"I don't know," said Mother as she continued with her cooking.

Mike pouted and thought about making a scene or having a temper tantrum. Instead, however, he went back into his room, pawed through the dirty clothes on the floor, and, taking the least soiled items, dressed himself. Then he put his other clothes in the hamper, filling it with almost two weeks' accumulation of dirty clothes. Later he went to the kitchen to have breakfast.

"When are you washing?" he asked Mother while eating.

"My usual day," Mother said. "Thursday."

"Could you do some today?" Mike asked.

"No," said Mother, gently but firmly.

"Why not?" Mike persisted.

Mother did not answer.

Mike got up, not finishing his breakfast, and went off to school.

Mother refused to wash his clothes before Thursday because she didn't want to give him special treatment; she wanted him to experience the logical consequences of his behavior. That night Mike washed his own socks—a rather messy procedure. The next day he went to school with a stained shirt. Mother was tempted to keep him home. She even thought of purchasing a new shirt for him but decided to let him learn and said nothing. When Thursday came, both Mother and Mike were practically in a state of exhaustion.

Thereafter Mother never found Mike's hamper empty on a Thursday morning.

One morning, as usual, Mrs. Goss and Evelyn, eight, got into a battle. "Evelyn, you'll catch cold and be sick if you don't wear your coat, hat, scarf, and boots; it's twenty degrees out there." Evelyn was strongly against wearing them, but at the end of the hassle she went off to school with all the clothes on her that Mother thought she needed.

Father thought this kind of battle was a nuisance, and he said to his wife, "Evelyn ought to know how she feels; maybe she just doesn't feel the cold as much as you do." But Mother knew best.

Next morning, as the daily battle was raging, the family doctor came to see Grandmother Goss, who was not well. Dr. Brown heard Mother stressing the need to wear heavy coats and bundle up if one wanted to avoid colds and not die of pneumonia. As he was leaving, Dr. Brown mentioned that he had heard the argument about clothes and added that colds do not come from cold weather but from viruses. Thus, in a few words, he demolished one of Mother's most cherished theories of health—a theory that still persists in folklore.

After the doctor had left, Mr. Goss put his foot down. He told Mother that she should not interfere with Evelyn's state of dress since Evelyn was an intelligent child, that perhaps she did not need as much clothing as others, and that in any case she should find out for herself what suited her best. And so Evelyn was allowed to choose her own clothes. She proceeded to go out in zero weather without her heavy coat. She returned from school blue and shivering, and Mother fully expected her to come down with a bad cold. But Evelyn did not get a cold all winter. After one more day of going coatless, she decided, without pressure from anyone, to dress appropriately for the weather. In fact, she started wearing just about the kind of clothing Mother thought she needed. Now, though, she was doing it *on her own.*

Every Sunday morning, almost without exception, there was a battle at the Slackman home. Whereas the other children dressed appropriately for church, little Susan insisted that she be allowed to wear jeans and a T-shirt. Sometimes Mother would forcibly dress Susan, who then yelled and cried; when they finally got to church, the whole family was feeling upset.

Mother was advised to let Susan wear whatever she wished, and the counselor suggested that Easter, which was coming soon, might be a good time to try this approach. Mother agreed reluctantly.

Easter morning, Mother told Susan, "You can wear what you want: your new white dress or your jeans and T-shirt." Surprised, Susan dressed in her everyday clothes, and the family drove off. Her brothers, Michael and Noah, were practically stiff in their brand-new clothes. At the church the parents got out of the car, then the children. When Susan saw how nicely all the other children were dressed, she climbed back into the car. The parents nodded at each other and went in to the service. The brothers went to the Sunday school. Susan stayed in the car. When the services were over, her parents said nothing about her dress or her behavior.

From then on, Susan was permitted to wear what she wanted—and she usually wanted to wear something appropriate to the occasion.

SUMMARY

In most cases, nagging about clothing is unnecessary. If at all feasible, let children wear what they select. They will quickly learn what is and what is not appropriate. By refusing to wash or clean clothes except when convenient to you, the parent; by refusing to purchase new clothes to replace clothes that have been mistreated; by wearing appropriate clothes yourself, you are doing your part. If a child dresses inappropriately, give your opinion—but go no further. Let the child learn to take responsibility for choosing what he wears. You show respect for the child when you let him dress his body with his own selection. However, you do not have to go out with him if you would feel uncomfortable at being seen with him because he is dressed so badly. You can always say, "You can dress this way; but if you do, I feel ashamed of your appearance and will not be seen with you." Do not say this, however, unless his appearance is such that you really would be mortified.

10 | *Eating*

"Hurry," Mother said to Peter. "Breakfast is getting cold." Reluctantly he came to the kitchen. She asked gaily, "How do you want your eggs?"

Peter frowned. "I don't want eggs."

"Now," Mother said wearily, "you know you need eggs; you need protein. And how about some Jumbies?" This was a reference to the popular cereal he had demanded a week ago.

"No," Peter answered. "I want Quickie Dickies." He knew she didn't have that cereal.

"How about Mumbo Tumbos or some Juicy Deucies?" the harried mother asked.

After several minutes of discussion and negotiation—he wanted pineapple juice and French toast—she finally managed to get a breakfast that appealed to him. The entire process took fifteen minutes of talk, fifteen of preparation, five for eating.

DISCUSSION

Dr. Dreikurs often said, "There is only one creature on earth that does not want to eat—the American child." The reasons are varied; one is the misconception, widespread among mothers, that a fat baby is a healthy one. This causes them to push food on their young child, trying, for instance, to get him to take "another bite for Mother" and then "another bite for Daddy." This is one of many games used to stuff a child. Mothers generally fear that their child will not take in each day the amounts and kinds of food that are best for him. Some even fear that their children may die from some kind of dietary deficiency.

In 1928, Davis* reported an experiment now considered a classic. It involved letting an experimental group of young children eat whatever they wanted. A matched comparison group of children were given dietetically selected foods. The results were interesting: the children who had been permitted to eat whatever they wished were taller, heavier, and healthier than their control mates. An examination of what these children had chosen to eat revealed some unusual feeding patterns. Some went on "fads" and for several meals would eat just one or two foods, perhaps cottage cheese, chocolate, milk, or chopped meat. Then they would go off this fad and perhaps not eat a previously favored food for a month. Some ate very little one day and three times as much the next day. But when their intakes were totaled, it was found that every child, even though any single meal may have been unbalanced, had achieved a balanced diet every week!

Meal times should be happy times. Parents have a right to enjoy their meals. Young children need some help, but parents should not give them too much service. It is so easy for Mother to slip into the habit of doing just that: to pour juice for the kids, to fill all the plates, and to run and get what family members request from the refrigerator or cabinet. She is then reduced virtually to the status of a servant, forever at the beck and call of her children. She must disengage herself from giving her children unnecessary service and must teach them to become self-sufficient as soon as possible.

SOLUTION

Parents can usually correct feeding problems rather quickly. They should keep these points in mind:
1. Feeding time should be pleasant.

* C. M. Davis, "Self-Selection of Diet of Newly Weaned Infants," *American Journal of Disease of Children*, 1928, pp. 36, 651–79.

2. Every child should decide for himself how much, if any, he is to eat of the foods Mother has prepared (if the demand for any dish exceeds the supply, the child must, of course, be limited to his fair share). He should be permitted to serve his own plate from serving dishes; when necessary, a parent may help him. The selection and the amount of food on his plate should be determined by the child without any comment from others.

3. Given enough time and freedom of choice, children will develop a taste for many foods. They start life eating only one thing—milk; at five they may like to eat two dozen things; at ten they may eat a hundred. An adult, of course, may like several hundred, including snails and eels. But children, especially younger ones, are usually traditionalists. One must expect them to be reluctant to try new things.

4. A child should not be expected to eat the same amount at each feeding. At one meal Charlie may eat four ounces and at the next, twelve.

5. Dessert should never be a reward. It may be placed in a small plate at each place setting at the beginning of the meal. If a child eats only his dessert, that is all right. Since it is a small portion, he'll soon be hungry.

6. Eating should be the child's business. Parents do not necessarily know best. The less parents worry about eating, the better for everyone.

7. When the family, except the problem eater, is through eating, all plates, including his, should be removed from the table. If he is not given between-meal snacks, he will be hungry at the next meal.

8. A very stubborn child may choose not to eat for several meals or even for several days. He should be served his meals with the other family members. No mention should be made of his eating or failing to eat. His plate should be removed when the rest of the family have finished. He should *not* be allowed snacks. If parents stick to this procedure, the child will eat eventually. No one can go very long without food.

SOLUTION APPLIED TO PETER

Peter's mother was in an Adlerian study group with other mothers. She learned our approach to feeding problems and discussed it with her husband and children. She then established the following routine: she rang a bell ten minutes before mealtime and again when the meal was to be served; everyone was then to come to the table. For this meal there was to be only this serving for everyone! Peter balked at the first breakfast served in this manner. After he went hungry for a few mornings, he then ate what Mother had prepared.

FURTHER EXAMPLES

The Smiths and their four children—eight, seven, four, and two—went to visit Mrs. Smith's parents, the Riggs, in a distant city. William, the four-year-old, told his grandmother upon arrival, "Nana, I only eat cereal," and proceeded to look through kitchen cabinets until he found a box of dry cereal. This he placed on the dinner table. During dinner the Smiths continuously argued with William, saying that he should eat the meat and vegetables. William continued to eat his cereal. Everyone was upset by the arguing.

The next morning Mrs. Smith was helping her mother fix breakfast. She started by asking each child what he wanted to eat. Grandmother Rigg was surprised but said nothing as her daughter prepared a different meal for each child.

To give the young couple a vacation from the children, the grandparents offered to baby-sit; and the pair left for a four-day visit with friends in a nearby town. Grandfather Rigg called the children and Grandmother together to plan the next few days. Each of the children was given an opportunity to suggest a fun activity. Grandmother said, "I need a little help so that I can have time to join the fun. I would like everyone to help me plan a breakfast menu." The children agreed to help her do it. William suggested cereal for the next morning; Grandmother wrote that on her list for Monday, the first day; she then asked John and Dick what they wished and listed their requests for the next two days. The baby made no requests; in fact, she did not seem to understand what was going on. Grandmother explained that on Monday she would fix cereal and everyone would eat that. On Tuesday she would serve bacon and eggs as John requested and on Wednesday pancakes and bacon as Dick wanted.

Monday's breakfast went well. Tuesday, William looked at the bacon and egg on his plate and started to complain, but no one paid attention to him and he ate no breakfast. On Wednesday, he stared at the pancakes and bacon on his plate for a while, then heaved a sigh and started to eat slowly. He quietly said to himself, "Pancakes aren't so bad," and cleaned his plate. From then on he ate all the meals Grandmother prepared.

Mother and Father complained to a family counselor that their three boys, eight, ten, and twelve, would not eat meat.* A pediatrician had assured them that the kids were physically normal. The counselor asked why such a fuss was made over eating. Mother explained that the proteins in meat were better than those in cheese and beans and that, anyway, kids should eat everything.

The counselor suggested that the parents tell the children once and *only* once that from now on they could eat or not eat meat as they pleased and that the parents would respect their decision. The parents did so, and all three boys said they chose not to eat meat.

The usual hassle at table, with Mother and Father pleading and cajoling the children to eat meat, stopped. Mother prepared meat for herself and her husband and only vegetable dishes for the children. Peace descended on the family.

Several weeks later, Mother bought five chickens, fried them, and arranged the pieces on a tray to serve to company. Just before the first guests were due to arrive, she glanced at the tray and something looked wrong. She counted chicken legs—sure enough, one was missing. She immediately called her husband and began a tirade: "Why couldn't you wait? Sneaking a leg! That isn't right. . . ." The startled husband proclaimed his innocence. It took only a few seconds for them to figure out the answer: one of the children had stolen a chicken leg! Husband and wife hugged each other and began laughing.

That was the end of the meat-eating problem. From that time on they noticed that meat was disappearing from the refrigerator—a slice of packaged ham or a hamburger that had been put away. And slowly the children began "testing" meat at the table. The parents were smart enough to say nothing, and within a month all three children were eating meat.

* This incident was recounted to us by Dr. Dreikurs.

SUMMARY

If parents would treat eating as natural, they would not reinforce the poor eating habits of their children by nagging and scolding. Parents are often overconcerned about their children's getting the correct kind and amount of nutrients. Forcing food upon a child usually brings on his counterattack—not eating. It is quite strange that most people admire trim and slim adults but prefer young children to be chubby. Good eating habits can be easily learned when meals are planned to give a balanced diet and children are allowed to eat what they wish from what is placed before them. Snacks should not be given to children who are problem eaters, but may be offered to children who eat their meals.

We believe that it is best to have an open kitchen: any child can eat whatever he wants whenever he wants, going to the refrigerator at any time and taking out anything except things clearly forbidden, such as bottled soda or desserts. The meal table then has to compete with the refrigerator and the pantry. If a child wants to eat catch-as-catch-can on his own, there is no cause for alarm. Very soon the child, especially if required to clean up and put dishes and utensils away, will realize that cooked meals regularly served are better than hastily executed peanut butter and jelly sandwiches. Kids learn by experience the value of home cooking.

We think these general rules make sense about food:

1. Parents should buy and prepare food that suits their budget and is convenient for them, with consideration for children's preferences, if feasible.

2. Children should serve themselves.

3. Children should decide for themselves, without discussion, how much to take from serving dishes. If one child avoids onions and another asparagus and a third pineapple—fine.

4. A child should usually be expected to finish what he takes. If he takes too much, the remainder may be saved for that child to eat the next day.

5. Dessert is not a reward. It may be eaten first or last.

6. During a meal there should be no comment or discussion about the child's eating.

11 | *Keeping Clean*

"Jeff, did you take your shower?" Mother shouted.

"No."

"Hurry, they'll be coming soon to get you. You know you can't go till you've had your shower."

Father put down his paper and said to Mother in exasperation, "Harriet, why do you have to fight with Jeff every day about showering?"

"I don't know. He's certainly not like Frances. I guess girls are naturally clean and neat. Jeff is so thoughtless; if I didn't remind him, he would never bathe or wash his face."

"Well, he's eleven. When will he ever learn?"

"I have no idea. Jeff! I don't hear that shower running!"

"Darn it!" Father said in disgust. "It's so unpleasant when you shout at him. You're after him all the time."

"Well, why don't *you* come up with the answer? I'm positive that if I didn't keep after him all the time, he'd just be black as pitch. And during the summer when he runs around a lot and sweats a lot and gets so dirty, he just has to have a daily bath or he will smell."

"Maybe it would be better if we let him reach that state," Father said wearily. "At least maybe that way we would have some peace."

DISCUSSION

Problems involving the bathroom—washing one's face, brushing teeth, flushing the toilet, taking a bath, drying off properly, and so on—arise in many families, and few parents know what to do. Usually parents talk, talk, talk. But it does little good. Most parents give up after a while; but some are more determined, and keep on investigating and asking questions. They check the toothbrushes after the children have left the bathroom, to see if they are wet. Some parents go so far as to check the contents of the toilet bowl: they have to examine urine and feces for color and shape; they feel negligent if they do not check *everything*.

SOLUTION

1. You, the parents, should have good toilet habits yourselves.
2. Instruct the children as to just what they should do (instruction may be by parents' example).
3. Check occasionally but do not conduct an FBI-type investigation.
4. The child should experience the natural or logical consequence of his behavior.
5. Tooth-brushing should be an issue between the child and the dentist and not between the child and the parents.
6. Meals should not be served to a child who has not washed his hands and face.
7. If the child does not bathe and smells bad, you can ask him to remove his plate and eat his meal away from you—in the kitchen, for instance, if you eat in the dining room. He should not make your meal unpleasant. However, if he is in a power contest with you, it is wiser for you and your spouse to remove your plates and eat elsewhere when he smells bad or looks dirty.

APPLICATION TO JEFF'S PROBLEM

"Let the child decide for himself," the family counselor said to the parents. "In this case, tell Jeff that from now on it will be his own decision whether or not to bathe."

The mother immediately disagreed. "I know my son. He just will not wash himself *ever*. Who knows what will happen?"

"What could happen?" the counselor asked.

"He would smell bad or something."

"So much the better," the counselor stated. "That may get him washing himself on his own. If he smells bad enough, others will tell him. This would be a natural consequence. From this he would learn."

The parents discussed the advice and decided to take it. They talked to their two children and part of the conversation went as follows:

"From now on, it is up to you to take a bath when you want. We'll no longer keep after you."

Both kids jumped up and down for joy. "I'll never take another bath again," Jeff said excitedly but firmly.

And it seemed he meant it because a week later, he still had not taken a bath. His skin was dirty and he definitely smelled bad. Mother tightened her fists and held herself back. Ten days later, she heard Jeff crying, and she went into his room. "What is it?" In answer he raised his left arm, and she saw along his body a line of small white pimples. "It hurts," he complained. "We'll go to the doctor," she said. "Get dressed." She was just about to tell him to take a bath before dressing to go to the doctor but decided instead to phone the counselor. His advice as to having Jeff wash was: "Don't."

"That is a condition that afflicts dirty people. You haven't taken any baths. Why? Is there a shortage of water?" asked the doctor later at his office.

"No. I asked our family counselor, and I was told to let him suffer the consequences if he didn't take a bath, and this is what happened."

"Well, young fellow, if you don't keep clean, you get this impetigo type of sore. No, there is no medication. Just keep yourself clean. That's all."

And from that day on, there was no trouble with Jeff about showering, except that every once in a while he would be in the shower too long and use too much hot water.

FURTHER EXAMPLES

Mrs. Johnson and her daughter Nancy would fight periodically about Nancy's not washing her hair. Finally the mother gave up the battle and said, "It's your hair." Nancy let her hair go. It got very oily and then began to smell. When other kids mentioned this, Nancy began to wash her hair.

Almost every night when the twins were told to wash, Mother or Father felt it necessary to come into the bathroom to urge them to hurry, stop playing, finish their bath, and go to bed. Sometimes Mother or Father washed them. The parents were told by the counselor to let the kids play as long as they wanted, to see what would happen. The parents agreed to go along with this. The first week the children were in the bathroom an average of forty minutes every night. The second week they averaged about twenty. The third week they averaged five.

The children had played excessively and dragged out their bath because the parents interfered. Once they had freedom to play, it was no longer as much fun, and so they cut down the time.

Dan did not take a bath for quite a while and began to smell bad. When his parents mentioned it, he got very angry. They felt uncomfortable eating with that odor, but they knew that Dan would be furious and would not leave on his own if told to eat in the kitchen—he would have to be dragged there, and he was a heavy eleven-year-old. The parents took their plates to their own room. There, for several days, they ate their meals. One evening, another family called to ask if Dan's family would join them in eating at a pizza place. Dan was left at home after the parents explained to him that they did not wish to inflict his odor on the friends or on others in the restaurant. They told him this only once, in a quiet, friendly way. Dan decided that very night to take baths —he really wanted to be with the family.

Mrs. Cleworth really had a thing going with her son Paul. She was keeping after him to brush his teeth. Practically every night she would harangue him about the importance of properly cleaning his teeth, how cavities would occur, and so forth. His younger brother, Sam, always brushed his teeth carefully. However, whenever they went to the dentist, it was Sam, the tooth-brusher, who usually had cavities, while Paul never had any. Paul used this fact as an argument against his mother's prodding.

And so Mrs. Cleworth consulted the dentist. He told her that no one really knew what caused cavities and that some researchers wondered whether tooth-brushing might not actually help bring them on. He himself believed that children *should* brush teeth but felt that gum massage was even more important. He informed her that there were people in their late seventies who had never had a toothache and had never brushed their teeth. "It's probably a matter of heredity, for the most part," he told her. "In any case, why make your child suffer about tooth-brushing? Let him get a cavity—that might make him brush his teeth. But I still think it is more heredity than anything else."

With that Mrs. Cleworth gave up, thinking: After all, they're *his* teeth. Let him suffer. Unfortunately, perhaps, he never did get any cavities. Anyhow, the battles were over—and that, the husband said, was a blessing.

SUMMARY

The bathroom should be the child's domain when he is in it. Constant supervision or battling is ineffective in training the child about cleaning up. These matters are the child's business. Parents have an obligation to be good examples—to keep themselves clean—and to instruct children in good toileting procedures; nagging and making a big issue about them is unecessary and unwise. The best general rule is to let the child experience the natural consequences of his behavior. Bit by bit the child will learn. One toothache can be a lifetime lesson.

12 | *School Difficulties at Home*

It had really been some day, Mrs. Thompson reflected as she waited for her husband to come home; some day indeed. About 9 A.M., the school clerk had called to say that Timmy, thirteen, had not yet arrived. When he and his sister Debra came home that afternoon, they brought their report cards. Timmy had two C's, two D's, and two F's. He had been late twenty-eight times and absent four times (as far as Mrs. Thompson could remember, he had been absent—for illness—only *two* days). Debra, ten, brought home one B, four C's, and one D. Attached to her report card was a note asking Mrs. Thompson to make sure that Debra would in the future come to school with her homework completed, and to please check her homework because Debra usually brought work to school that looked as though she had given it only about ten minutes' attention. And then, to cap everything, Mrs. Thompson found a note in the mail about her youngest child, Ted, five, still in kindergarten, asking Mrs. Thompson if she would please take him to a doctor because he might require medical attention since he found it so difficult to sit still and to follow directions.

What a situation! Mrs. Thompson reflected. How will my husband react?

* This incident was recounted to us by Mrs. Bronia Grunwald.

DISCUSSION

Similar school-related situations occur in millions of American families and are generally considered by the parents to be matters of the utmost importance. Most parents are eager to do anything in their power that they think will help their child's schooling. Indeed, many seem to consider themselves and the home to be virtually an extension of the school system. They check to make sure that the child does the homework, and then they double-check to make sure it is done correctly. There is great concern over report cards, and children are gravely warned about not being able to go to college if they have low grades.

What should parents do—and *not do*—at home to help their child at school?

SOLUTION

Our answer to this question is in two parts: one deals with improving the attitude of the child; the other with improving the attitude of the parent.

Parents should motivate the child to study and to enjoy learning.

Lecturing is generally useless, such as telling him that school is necessary for success or happiness, or making comparisons between him and other people's children, or recounting all the mistakes you, the parent, made in your own education. There are other, more effective things you can do:

At table, talk about interesting intellectual subjects, such as religion, politics, history, science, art, music. Search newspapers and magazines and "bone up" on topics for discussions. If the children venture opinions, encourage them to talk by listening to them.

Take courses yourself, whether it be in basket-weaving at the local YMCA or in the history of philosophy at the nearest university extension department. Do your homework in plain sight, and discuss your courses.

Subscribe to magazines that are intellectual and interesting to children as well as to adults, such as *National Geographic* or *Scientific American*. Hang really good art around the house rather than calendar-type art; get good music on records and tapes, and play them.

Invite people over, and try to lead the discussion away from topics such as what's on television or who committed the latest local nuisance.

Have at hand books, encyclopedias, atlases, almanacs, and other reference matter.

A good globe of the earth is helpful. A telescope for searching the heavens at night and a microscope for examining water, leaves, and insects will stimulate interest in the world of nature. Toys of an educational and scientific nature, such as chemistry sets, can be quite worthwhile.

Educational play can be started in infancy. Games such as Scrabble are of value in alerting children to the use of vocabulary.

Take them to plays and operas.

Encourage them in every way you can to enter the world of the intellect.

In short, if you want your children to become interested in learning, the best way is to lead them, not to direct or force them. By forcing you will make them hate school, but by leading it is *possible* that you may awaken interest in education. If a child has already established other interests, or if he has low intellectual potential, even these steps may fail. In any case, don't forget this: the sure way to fail to make children *want* to do something is to try to force them.

What attitude should the parent take about school?

1. To the very limit that is feasible, let school be the child's business. He is going to school primarily for his own sake, not for yours.

2. To the very limit that is feasible, let the school handle the child's schooling—let the specialists teach him and guide him. Except in very exceptional circumstances, your interference is more likely to harm than to help.

3. Do not do the school's work even if school personnel ask you to. Gently refuse to involve yourself in conflicts between the child and the school. Refuse to check the child's homework, or to urge him to do it by a certain time.

4. Do not do his work for him, but do help if he requests you to

quiz him on spelling, multiplication tables, and the like. Direct him to reference sources, rather than serving as an information agency. "How do you spell 'quickly'?" the child asks. Mother should suggest that he look up the word in the dictionary.

5. Do not reward or punish the child for his schoolwork. If he gets good grades, do not go into raptures; if he gets poor grades, do not criticize him.

6. Do, however, show interest in the child's schoolwork. Ask questions about what he is learning, and be ready to see him demonstrate his work—such as getting a square root.

7. Join and be active in your Parent-Teacher Association. Be concerned about the kind of school you have.

SOLUTION APPLIED TO THE
THOMPSONS' PROBLEM

After a session with a counselor, Mrs. Thompson had a talk with the children.

"From now on, school is your business. I will not get involved anymore with your schoolwork. If you have homework, it is up to you to do it—I'll not remind you to do it, nor will I check it. I repeat: *school is your business from now on.* Do you understand?"

"Will you help me when I can't do my homework?" Debra asked.

"No," said Mother. "Homework will be your problem, not mine. If you pay attention in school you will learn what to do. I want you to get a good education, but I will not do your work for you."

Mother had a talk with the teacher too, when she called to say that Debra was not doing her homework.

"I am sorry," Mrs. Thompson said, "but I have been advised to no longer supervise Debra's schoolwork. I am afraid it will have to be between you and Debra."

"But, Mrs. Thompson," Miss Fujiwara complained, "she just doesn't do her homework, and you *should* check it."

"I am just not going to do that anymore. You're her teacher, and you have my permission to do whatever you wish to get her to do her work. I am responsible for her behavior at home and her chores here, but *you* have to make sure she takes care of her schoolwork. Give her poor grades, keep her in late, even fail her at the end of the year if she doesn't do her work. I am completely through with checking to see if she has homework or if she has done it right or anything like that. School is her business and your business. The more I interfere, the worse it is for her."

Mrs. Thompson spoke also to little Ted's teacher: "I'm sorry, Mrs. Redwin, that my Ted doesn't behave himself in kindergarten. If you cannot handle him, just return him and I'll keep him at home. I will not take him to a doctor to have him drugged. My pediatrician says that he is an active, high-spirited, normal boy and that if he doesn't adjust to your school it is not necessarily his fault but may be the school's—or that maybe he is simply not ready to go to school. As a matter of fact, I have some retraining for Ted at home. I believe our new way of handling the children with logical consequences will help him to learn to sit still for longer periods."

Mrs. Thompson told her husband: "From now on, as far as I'm concerned, school is the kids' problem. I'll just make sure they have the supplies they need, like books, pencils, and paper. I'll make sure they don't stay home when they should be in school. I won't bug them about homework or make a big fuss about their grades. When report cards are brought home, I'll sign them without comments, unless the children ask for them. I'll go to PTA meetings and see if I can't change things about so that instead of excessive concern with things like buying equipment for the football team there will be some attention to this kind of schooling the children are receiving.

As a result of Mrs. Thompson's new attitude, the kids began to get better grades and to behave better in school. Mrs. Thompson found that she now had more time to do other things, and she started some formal learning of her own—with a Great Books study group—and increased her pleasure in intellectual discussions.

FURTHER EXAMPLES

A mother called a counselor after her sixteen-year-old son had struck his father and run away. The dispute had been about school. When the parents came to the counselor for an interview, the father raged about his son, saying that the boy was interested only in playing, did not study, did not do schoolwork, brought home poor grades, would not be able to enter a good college, etc.

The counselor interviewed father and son together on a subsequent date. The father repeated his complaints; the son expressed disinterest in school and showed great resentment of his father for many years of harassment about school.

The counselor advised that from now on the father should completely disregard the son's schooling, and leave it up to the boy. The son was delighted with the advice, and the father finally agreed reluctantly to take it.

The boy stopped attending school, got a job, and worked for a year. He then took examinations for entering college but made very low scores. He enrolled at night school, worked hard on his academic deficiencies, took the examinations again, and passed them. He then went to college and now is doing well there.

When the counselor interviewed the youth again, he said, "I think now that my father was right, but I just wouldn't listen to him. That year I worked showed me that education is important. But—I had to find out for myself."

Mrs. Richman was a very good mother. Every night she helped her son with his schoolwork. She was most concerned that he do well in school. He was quite docile and learned quickly. Yet his teacher kept reporting that he was uncooperative and inattentive. Mrs. Richman finally said to the teacher, "I can't understand why he pays attention to me but not to you."

The teacher replied, "If you didn't try to do my job, if you would stop tutoring him, perhaps he'd pay more attention to me."

That possibility had never occurred to Mrs. Richman, but the suggestion seemed to make sense. So she stopped helping her son and told him that school was the place for him to look for assistance in his schoolwork. Sure enough, in a short time her son began to pay attention in school. Why would he pay attention in school as long as he had a private tutor at home?

Irving's father was sick of his son's poor grades and said to him, "I'll give you a hundred dollars for every A you bring home." Two months later, the son brought to his father a report card with five A's.

"Where's my five hundred dollars?" the boy asked, for he had a minibike all picked out.

"Here is five bucks," the father said. "I was kidding about giving you one hundred dollars. I just wanted to see whether you could get an A if you really tried. And now I know you can if you want to."

"Well, next report card I'll have all F's. I'll show you."

And that is exactly what happened.

Richard quit school at fifteen, in his first year of high school, to work for his father on the farm. At seventeen he volunteered for the army, and there he served for six years. At twenty-three, he passed the GED examination. He went through college in three years and medical school in four, and at thirty was an M.D.

SUMMARY

One of the most serious and common errors by parents is interference in their children's schooling. Parents should try to motivate them indirectly by creating an intellectual atmosphere in the home rather than directly by lecturing and criticizing, by punishing and praising.

School is, and should be, the child's business. Do not help him, do not supervise, do not criticize. Depend on the child's natural desire to improve himself. And remember: higher education is not a must for everyone.

13 | *Bedtime*

A young couple named Schuetz had two children: a seven-year-old boy and a five-year-old girl. The parents were teachers in an elementary school in a residential area. The Schuetzes lived on the school ground in a large dwelling with three other families. An overriding concern of the Schuetz couple was to not disturb the others in the dwelling. They lived there rent-free and intended to save enough money eventually to buy a home of their own.

The big problem was bedtime. Because of their concern that the children's crying would disturb others and also because of their faulty concepts about sleep, a typical schedule from about 7 P.M. to 7 A.M. ran as follows:

7:00 P.M.—Mother would ask the children to put on their pajamas and get ready for bed. There would be squabbling.

7:30—Mother would take the kids to the bathroom, wash them one at a time, and supervise their tooth-brushing.

8:00—The parents would don pajamas. Father would go into the son's bedroom and read to him for a half hour. Mother would do the same with the daughter.

8:30—Father would leave the son and re-dress himself. Mother would lie on the bed with the daughter and stay there for about a half hour until the child fell asleep. Mother would then re-dress herself.

10:30—The parents themselves would go to bed.

1:00 A.M.—The daughter would get up and awaken Mother, who would then take the girl to the bathroom, wait while she urinated, take her back to her bed, and lie down with her until the girl fell asleep again.

2:00—The boy would come to the parents' room and wake up the father, who would take the boy to the bathroom and then tuck him in bed.

4:00—The daughter would get up and go to the parents' room and get into bed with them.

5:00—The son would enter the parents' bed, and the father would get up and go to finish his sleep in the son's bed.

7:00—The parents would get up.

DISCUSSION

While the above situation is highly unusual, bedtime problems are quite common—and usually completely unnecessary. Frequently, problems arise from misconceptions. Many parents do not realize that no one knows just how much sleep is needed by, say, a ten-year-old. It is wrong to try to make a child sleep a certain number of hours. Each individual must find, by experience, how much sleep he needs. On this point even twins may differ considerably from each other. Jim, ten, may usually sleep ten hours while his twin sister, Susie, gets along fine with eight.

Sometimes we encounter a child who has no idea that sleep is a physiological necessity. He knows only that his parents impose a bedtime on him, which he believes is unfair, and he feels that he has a right to fight with them about this issue. Some parents believe that their child would never get enough sleep unless they arbitrarily set hours for his sleeping; they make rules, nag, threaten, spank— all to no avail.

SOLUTION

Our suggestions for solving bedtime problems should work within a week—if you, the parent, follow them consistently.

1. By discussion with the children, find the time they think they should go to bed. Usually children are more reasonable on this point than the parent might expect. They may say eight-thirty if bedtime has previously been eight. If they decide that they want to stay up so late that you and your spouse would have no time to be alone together, you can tell them that they must be *in their room* by an appointed hour, because you would enjoy some time to yourselves.

2. Explain that they must stay in their room, that they may have the light either on or off, and that they may go to sleep whenever they wish. You should *not* lie down with a child to "help" him fall asleep.

3. After they are in their room, they may call you to read a story or simply to tuck them in. Then they may sleep or stay awake, but they must stay in their room.

4. If the child comes out of the room, quickly take him back in, *in silence*. If he again comes out, again take him back quickly in silence. Continue as long as necessary. Stay near the bedroom door if necessary.

5. See that the child gets up at his regular time. If he is tired, so much the better. He should not be allowed to sleep late if he has stayed up too late the night before.

6. If a child has to go to the bathroom during the night, do not accompany him. Keep a very weak light on in the hall and bathroom. He can go by himself.

7. Do not allow a child to get into your bed except when you want him to. For example, you may invite him to come into your bed any weekend morning by leaving your bedroom door open. If from the start you do not allow his sleeping in your bed, he will go along with that. If he has already trained you to accept him in your bed, tell him—but only once—that it disturbs your sleep and that you will no longer allow it. If, after being told, he does disturb your sleep, lock your bedroom door to keep him out. You will not have to lock the door more than once or twice.

8. If a child has a bad dream or is afraid of the dark, do not pay a lot of attention to it. See Chapter 27, in which we discuss this in detail.

9. Do not make a big fuss over sleep, for that may cause the child to develop undesirable sleep habits that persist into adulthood.

SOLUTION APPLIED TO THE SCHUETZ FAMILY

Following their counselor's instructions, the Schuetzes went to their adult neighbors and explained what they were going to do to solve their problem. The neighbors applauded them for seeking professional advice and assured them that if the children cried for a time it would not annoy them. Armed with this assurance, the Schuetzes had a talk with the kids and told them that from now on they had to be in their bedroom by eight-thirty but that if they wished, Father and Mother would come in for a few minutes to say good night or read a story. From now on they were to go to the bathroom by themselves. They would be allowed to get into their parents' bed only on Sunday and holiday mornings. The daughter announced that if Mother didn't sleep with her she would cry. Mother, who had been forewarned about children's tendencies to blackmail, merely said, "Well, go ahead and cry if you want."

That night, at precisely eight-thirty, both kids were taken to their rooms. To the surprise of their parents, neither cried. About nine, the son called for Father to tell him a story; this the father did gladly. The little girl did not ask for a story. Eventually the kids went to sleep, and the parents retired. About one o'clock, as per her usual schedule, the girl appeared at Mother's side of the bed, but the mother refused to get up. The girl began to cry. Mother, following the counselor's instructions, got out of bed, pulled the child out of the bedroom, and closed the door (but didn't lock it). The girl cried for about five minutes, then went to bed. About two o'clock, the boy showed up at his father's side and just waited there, saying nothing. Father did not get up. Eventually, the son went back to his room. At 4 A.M., the girl tried to get in bed on Mother's side, and Mother pushed her out. She then tried to get in on Father's side, and he pushed her out. She then crawled in at the foot of the bed. Father picked her up—all this in silence—and put her out of the room, closing the door. Again she cried, but she went to her room. The boy did not show up for his usual 5 A.M. visit.

Within two more days the problem was completely solved. On Sunday, having been reminded by the parents the night before, both kids were welcomed into the parents' bed by 7 A.M.

Larry, two and a half, stubbornly sat down on the kitchen floor when his divorced mother said it was bedtime. But Mother had learned about logical consequences from a counselor: she went into her own bedroom, closed the door, and read until she fell asleep. The next morning she found Larry asleep on the kitchen floor. She said nothing to him about the incident. Thereafter Larry went to bed at the proper time since he realized he would not get a payoff (attention or a fight) for refusing to go to bed.

Four-year-old Greg and his mother came to our Family Education Center. Mother told the counselor that Greg would not go to bed on time, that they had a fight on this matter every night. The counselor talked with Greg while Mother was out of the room.

Counselor: Mother says that you don't want to go to bed at night.

Greg: That's right.

C: How late would you like to stay up?

G: Late.

C: As late as the news on TV?

G: Yes.

C: As late as when TV goes off the air?

G: Sure.

C: All night?

G: Yes.

C: How many nights?

G: Three.

C: O.K. You may stay up for three nights. You are not to get into your bed, but you may use the couch in the living room.

G: O.K.

Mother was told to allow Greg to stay up and to tell Father about the plan.

A few days later, she called the counselor to report: Greg had slipped into his bed during each of the three nights. They had no more problems with Greg about bedtime. He had learned that sleep is a necessity.

In the Overholt family, bedtime had always been a problem.

Both David and Betty, eight and nine, fought every night to stay up later than the time the parents had arbitrarily set as bedtime. After consulting a counselor, the parents made the following agreement with the kids: They could stay up as long as they wanted, but if, after 8:30 P.M., the children got into a fight or if either of them acted up, the disturbing party or parties would be sent to their rooms and had to remain there until it was time to get up in the morning. The children gladly agreed to this arrangement and there was no trouble for several nights. The kids were staying up late and awakening rather tired in the morning, but the parents were not unduly alarmed—the counselor had said they could expect the kids sooner or later to set up their own good bedtime schedule.

About eight forty-five one evening a week after this routine was started, the children got into a fight. Father immediately told them to go to their rooms. Betty went at once; but David refused and said he wanted to see the rest of the TV program. In silence, Father carried David to his room and put him in it with a pleasant "Good night." A minute later, David was back in the living room, looking at the TV. Father quickly carried him back again in silence. Within thirty seconds David came again to the living room. And this time when Father started to take David back to his room, David began to resist. Father said nothing but put him back in his room and then remained by the door. When David came out, Father, saying nothing, firmly but gently put him back inside. In the next half hour they went through this procedure about a dozen times. Father never lost his temper, and he remained friendly in manner. Finally, David got the message; he remained inside and went to sleep.

This sort of thing never happened with Betty, but David tested the situation several more times before he realized that Father or Mother would make him live up to their contract.

Within a month both children set their own bedtime routines; and these, as was evident from their appearance each morning, gave them ample rest.

SUMMARY

Many parents do not trust their children to act intelligently; this in effect shows that they lack respect for them. If given the chance, a normal child will show himself to be watchful, wary, and sensible. He is quite capable of learning by experience how much sleep he needs and of seeing to it that he gets it. By so doing, he learns to take responsibility for himself.

III | PROBLEMS OF ORDER AND COOPERATION

For a family to be happy, cooperation is necessary. If one person does less than his share, he puts a burden on the others. If he does more than his share, he is letting the others take advantage of him. In some families, one member is virtually a slave, while another lolls about not doing his fair share.

How can one get a child to cooperate? How can one get a child to do chores if he absolutely refuses? If a child wants to be sloppy, how can one get him to help keep the house fairly straight and clean? What about that especially difficult area, the child's own room? Is there a way, without screaming at children, without threats or spankings, to get them to do their fair share of keeping the house in order?

Yes, there is. By patient and persistent use of natural and logical consequences, children can be led to become cooperative. Even if your children are spoiled and have never done a lick of work in the house, you can, if you really make up your mind, succeed in training them. So gird up your loins. You have a fortnight of hard work ahead of you, but you'll find the effort indeed worthwhile.

14 | *Conformance*

Mrs. Fisher was having a cup of coffee in her living room with her neighbor Mrs. Kozuma. Suddenly, hearing a slight noise, Mrs. Fisher jumped up and ran into the kitchen. A moment later, the neighbor heard Mrs. Fisher shouting, "No, no, no!" Then came the sounds of a slap and a loud wailing. Mrs. Fisher came from the kitchen leading her two-year-old, Linda, by the wrist while the little darling screamed bloody murder. "You keep out of the kitchen," Mrs. Fisher said sternly to Linda, "and keep out of the cabinet!" After this admonition, she kissed her squalling child and pushed her out into the yard.

"What was all that about?" Mrs. Kozuma asked.

"I just can't make that child obey. I don't want her to go into the kitchen."

"Why not? What's wrong with the kitchen?"

"Linda always opens my cleaning cabinet. I have all kinds of dangerous things in it: ammonia, soap powders, bleaches, cleaners. I must have told her a thousand times to keep out of it, but she's so stubborn. Really! I have never known a child quite like her. How do you make a child understand that you mean it when you say 'No'?"

"I don't know. I guess every child is different. Mine went through disobedient stages, but Harry was the most difficult," said the older woman.

Mrs. Fisher went on, "My husband says that I should slap her hard every time, that I don't hit her hard enough, but you can't go around slapping a two-year-old. She just doesn't understand. I don't want her to hate me."

"And you can't really reason with a two-year-old. I guess you just have to always be alert and know where they are at all times to keep them out of mischief," the neighbor replied.

DISCUSSION

To get one's child to conform to one's wishes may seem difficult or even impossible. Parents often complain that their children do not comply when asked to do something or when told not to do something. By their defiant attitudes, children at times almost seem to ask to be punished.

We *can* scare a child into obedience; we *can* punish a child into compliance. But these methods may cause undesirable character traits—may produce a fearful, sly, or hostile child. What can parents do to produce children who will obey reasonable orders but are self-confident and resourceful?

SOLUTION

1. **Minimize the necessity for orders.** It is best, if possible, to arrange matters so that the parent does not have to give orders. If you don't keep a loaded pistol on the coffee table, you will not have to tell the child not to touch it. You should, so to speak, "childproof" your house. If you put expensive, fragile things away, you avoid many unnecessary problems with young, exploring children. This is a common-sense solution.

2. **When feasible, make a request instead of giving an order.** An order must be obeyed; a request gives the child a choice.

3. **Make unmistakably clear to the child what he is expected to do or not to do.** There should never be room for doubt or misunder-

standing as to the requirements or limitations being imposed upon him.

4. **Explain to the child the consequences of his failure to comply.**

5. **Obtain the child's agreement to the requirements or limitations.**

6. **If the child violates the agreement,** the consequences should follow *immediately.* The parent's role in the consequences should be played in *absolute silence.*

7. **A second chance** may be given if the child is again willing to make the same agreement and thinks that he is old enough to follow through.

8. **If he violates the agreement a second time,** he again suffers the consequences and must wait a longer time for another chance.

9. **For a third attempt,** he should be asked if he now thinks he is old enough to try again. If he says that he does but again violates the agreement, use logical consequences for a longer period of time. You can let him try again at a later time—usually several days later.

10. **Since the child wants the desired circumstances,** he will soon learn that he will be allowed them only if he complies with the requirements or limitations as defined by the parents and agreed to by himself.

The child learns by this method to choose desirable behavior instead of misbehavior. He learns to make good decisions and will become a more responsible adolescent and adult.*

APPLICATION TO THE KITCHEN CABINET INCIDENT

Let us now return to Mrs. Fisher. She went to an Adlerian family counselor and explained her problem with the kitchen cabinet and two-year-old Linda.

Counselor: You are in effect rewarding Linda when she opens

---

* We do not suggest this method for training adolescents.

that cabinet. She gets you involved with her. If she is lonely, or bored, or wants your attention, she knows just what to do—she opens the cabinet, and you drop everything to "play with her."

Mrs. Fisher: Play with her? I do just the opposite!

C: But is that how she sees it? We have to see matters from the child's point of view. Your behavior is reinforcing her behavior even though your intention is just the opposite.

F: You mean I cause her to misbehave by giving her attention? How else can I get her to stop opening that kitchen cabinet and rummaging in it?

C: I'll tell you exactly what to do. This method usually works quickly with very young children. We assume that the child wants attention from you and that you give it to her when you talk to her, telling her not to do it again, spanking her, and so on. True, the attention you give is unpleasant, but perhaps she would rather have that than get no attention at all.

F: Do you think that I should give her attention in other ways —that if she gets favorable attention for other things she may stop misbehaving?

C: While I do recommend attention for useful behavior, that in itself will not stop poor behavior. I suggest you make a contract with her: "If you behave yourself in the kitchen, you can go into it; but if you don't behave, you can't."

F: How do I enforce that?

C: Get a gate, perhaps one of the type that opens up like scissors, and put it on the door of the kitchen. Then, when you are in the kitchen, if she opens the cabinet you can put her on the other side of the gate, telling her she has to stay out until she is old enough not to go into the cabinet.

F: I see. I am to take her out of the kitchen and close the gate behind her.

C: Right. But this is important: you must remove her *pleasantly and in absolute silence.* And one more thing: *do it as soon as she does something you don't want her to do.*

F: O.K. I can do that.

C: Do you know why I emphasize silence and speed?

F: No, not really.

C: First, *speed.* She should learn that misbehavior brings immediate unpleasant results: exile! Second, *silence.* She is likely to think you do not like her if you yell at her or even just speak disapprovingly to her, and she may begin to not like you. Let her learn that your behavior when she does undesirable things is rapid and friendly. In this way she will learn that it is her misbehavior (not Mother's anger) that leads to the undesirable results for her: the logical consequences.

F: Suppose, after she's taken out, she asks to come in and promises not to do it again?

C: We communicate with children only when we and the child are calm. If she is crying and sobbing and saying that she won't do it again, don't answer her; just go about your work. After she stops crying, you can talk with her and ask her in a quiet voice, "Do you want to come into the kitchen? Do you think you are old enough not to go into the cabinet?" And if she says "Yes," you say "O.K., come into the kitchen. I am glad to hear that you are a big girl." Then let her in. If she opens the cabinet, even one-eighth of an inch—out she goes again, rapidly and in silence. If you do not let yourself get upset but faithfully and consistently follow the procedure I have outlined, it is practically sure to work.

A week later, the counselor and Mrs. Fisher met again.

C: How did it go?

F: Fine. She no longer goes into the cabinet. I followed your suggestion. I told her once: "From now on, Linda, you may be in the kitchen only if you are old enough to stay out of the cabinet. If you open it, you must stay out of the kitchen until you grow old enough to stay out of the cabinet." She looked at me kind of oddly, because I wasn't angry when I said it. And she didn't touch it at all for two days. Usually she's at it five or ten times a day. She certainly understands more than I'd thought. The third day, she just started to open the cabinet and I immediately put her out of the kitchen, behind a chair I used as a barrier. She cried. When she quieted down, I asked her if she was old enough now. She said "Yes," so I let her into the kitchen. She tried again at the cabinet about fifteen minutes later. So I put her out again. Then I didn't let her back into the kitchen for the rest of the day. Finally, the next day she decided she was old enough, and she hasn't bothered with that cabinet since. I think I've licked the problem.

C: Congratulations, but you may be wrong. She may test you again. Usually, when you use Adlerian training techniques, they work right away but after a week or two the child mounts a second offensive—so you can expect that there will be another flare-up of this problem. And you must do exactly the same things the moment she starts again—if she does. Rapidly, silently, no anger, etc.

F: I think I understand, and what's more, I can see how I might apply this theory to other things. Thank you.

FURTHER EXAMPLES

The client was a heavy-set, gray-haired woman, and she told her problem to the Adlerian psychologist in a weary, discouraged way.

"My husband and I have four children. The oldest is twenty-two and is married. We have a daughter, twenty-one, who goes to college and a nineteen-year-old son, who lives with us. Our fourth is only five. He was a change-of-life baby; we did not plan to have him. We love him, of course, but he's so different from my other three. He's driving my husband and me up the wall. You see, we bought this house we live in soon after we were married, almost twenty-five years ago. Since then the city has grown and now a highway runs right in front of our house. A lot of families have moved away, but we really don't want to move. Still, we may have to move because of Donald—our five-year-old."

"What is the problem?"

"He likes to run across the street. It's like a game. No sooner is he out of the house than he darts into the street; since it has heavy traffic, this is extremely dangerous. My husband, my other son, and I have tried everything we can to stop him—we've talked to him, we've tried to bribe him, we've punished him, we've kept him in the house for days—but he's like a little maniac: his one aim in life seems to be to cross that street. He's just a little fellow but he has a will of iron. We keep the whole house locked up all the time. We have snap locks on every door, we keep the windows locked, the screens screwed in. If a door is ever left open, he sneaks out. We just can't trust him."

"This is certainly serious. Let me give you a complete program for training him.

"Step one: Talk to Donald. Take him out of the house and show him the exact limits within which he is permitted to move: how far he can go west—up to the curb; how far north, south, and east. Make sure that he understands these limits. Question him to make sure he knows how far he can go.

"Step two: Ask him if he wants to play outside.

"Step three: If he says 'Yes,' ask him if he feels he is old enough to stay within the allowed areas. If he says 'Yes' to that, ask him to tell you what is the farthest he will go in every direction—and only if he tells you or shows you the limits are you to let him out. Do not let him out unless he assures you he will not cross what ever boundaries you and he have established. If he refuses to make the agreement, don't let him out. When he does agree, let him out and watch him carefully, preferably from a place where he cannot see you—perhaps through a window. Have on your sneakers.

"Step five: If he crosses any boundary, run out and get him as quickly as you can and in *complete silence* bring him into the house. You can grab him by the wrist or the shoulder but say nothing at all. Don't look angry or upset. You want him to blame his misbehavior, not your anger, for the unpleasantness that is happening to him.

"Step six: Once in the house, he may ask you why you brought him in; he may deny crossing the boundary; he may have a temper tantrum—but you are not to respond in any way. When he is calm, say to him that he may go out if he wants to, and then once again go over the boundaries with him. Then tell him—and please use these exact words if you can remember them—'If you don't stay where you should, I will bring you in again and you can't go out again today. We'll have to wait until you are older and can act like a big boy.' Then give him his second chance. When he goes outside, again you look out the window. If he stays within the boundaries, fine; if not, take him in immediately in silence, and he stays in for the rest of the day. The next day, go through the same routine, but this time give him only one chance."

The mother followed this program exactly as suggested. In three days the little boy was playing outside the house and not crossing the street. In the next two weeks, however, he did try twice to cross it, and each time he was brought in for the rest of the day. He then stopped trying to cross it. He knew that he could not go out if he did.

This procedure has worked with hundreds of little children who had had trouble staying where parents wanted them to stay.

Mrs. Jones was a divorcee with two children, Mark, six, and Beth, eight. Her problem was unusual: twice she had to give up an apartment because of the noise her children made. She informed us that after losing the second apartment she had to send her children to her mother because she could not get suitable housing. While with Grandmother, the children were extremely upset and bitterly regretted the misbehavior that had caused the loss of their own place. After six months in which they constantly pleaded to be allowed to go back, their mother did succeed in getting an apartment, and she and the children were reunited. Sadly she informed us that her new landlord had the other day come to see her to tell her that he would file a dispossess notice if she did not keep the children quiet—that all the neighbors were complaining about their noise.

Whenever the mother in any way opposed the will of either of the children, either or both would back up against a wall and hammer on it with their elbows or bang a chair against the floor. This, of course, was blackmail, pure and simple: they knew their poor mother would do almost anything not to have the neighbors disturbed. She was at the mercy of tyrant children. If she attacked one, the other banged, and if she went after the banger, the other would make noise until she promised them whatever they wanted.

The mother explained to us that she felt torn between sorrow for her children because they had no father and desire to send them away. She felt completely defeated by them.

We suggested the bathroom technique (see page 26), but it did not work—the children made such a racket while Mother was in the bathroom that she came flying out to give in to whatever they wanted. We then advised her to tell the children that henceforth she would act as follows: if they started banging *she would run out of the house,* regardless of time, weather, or her condition of dress.*

* For a similar solution to an adult problem see R. J. Corsini, *Roleplaying in Psychotherapy* (Chicago: Aldine Publishing Co., 1966) pp. 17–20.

And this she did the very day she was given the advice. At dinner the kids started banging because she had no dessert for them. She got up from the table and away she went—down the stairs, into the street. The two kids followed her, crying, telling her that they wouldn't make any more noise; but she kept on going. This infuriated the children so that they banged on cars, walls of houses, etc. She walked and walked until both she and the children had calmed down, and then they all returned home. That same evening, when she was about to go to bed, the kids started banging again. She grabbed a dressing gown, threw it over her pajamas, and ran down the stairs, again followed by her kids. And again she led them on a very long walk that lasted for hours, refusing to listen to them, just walking, walking, walking. The three finally got home about midnight, with the two kids exhausted. For several days there was no banging, but one evening they started doing it again. As it happened, a near-hurricane was blowing that night. Out went Mother, without raincoat or umbrella, but this time the kids did not follow her. She walked in the rain to a café, where she had several cups of coffee and a long, long conversation with a friend. She returned home several hours after she had left. And this was the last time she had any problem with her children about noisemaking.

The mother of a retarded boy, seven, reported that he never did what he was told. To prove this, she called her son; he didn't even look up. "You see," she said, "he just doesn't pay attention to me." She said she worried that someday there might be a dangerous situation and that he wouldn't listen to her call and would get hurt.

The counselor advised the mother to do as follows: She was to call the child *in a low voice* and then, if he did not *immediately* come to her, she was to *run* to him and drag him to where she had been—and each time she did this, she was to do it with increasing firmness. The first six times she called him, she had to drag him to her chair, but the seventh time he got up and came over. During the next hour, the mother called the boy several more times. Each time he came quickly. Mother was told that from now on she must never call the boy unless she really wanted him. If he should disobey, she should make him mind by proper action; and if she could not think of any proper action, not to give him an order in the first place. But she was never to repeat an order!

The mother was almost in tears at this point. She called her son again and, when he came over, stroked his head and said, "I can hardly stand it. For the first time in his life he listens to me and comes when I call."

SUMMARY

At times it is necessary to have a child obey promptly, without question. A child will do that only if demands on him are few and if he trusts the parent, knowing that the latter will give a sudden command only for sufficient reason, such as impending danger. In general, it is wise to make very few demands, and, when possible, to make a request rather than to give an order. It is important to remember that we do not want to make robots who jump to any command. However, when parents do feel it necessary to give orders, the general advice given here should work with children below the age of twelve. *With teen-agers this method usually will not work.*

15 | *Chores*

The Vernon family—parents and five boys, six to fourteen—came to be interviewed at a Family Education Center. The parents, it soon became clear, had no control over their children. They awakened the boys in the morning and then fought with them throughout the day—to make them eat properly, do chores, do homework, stop fighting, share the television, get off the telephone, clean their rooms, use their toothbrushes, take baths, go to bed on time. The parents ranted and raved; the kids didn't even pay attention.

During the children's interview, they elbowed each other, went into paroxysms of laughter, tickled and batted each other around like five mad clowns. The counselor was unable to talk to them since any attempt to get their attention led to further clowning, so they were asked to leave.

Everyone felt sympathetic toward the parents. They were asked what single change would be most helpful.

Father: Cooperation, just plain cooperation. These kids don't do a thing to help out.

Counselor: What have you done to try to get them to cooperate?

Father: Everything we can think of. My wife and I work. We leave at 6 A.M. and we come home at 6 P.M. We do the shopping. My wife does the cooking and I do the cleaning. They just don't do anything—except laughing and giggling. If I hit one of them, they all cry like mad, jumping up and down, the whole lot of them. We tried a policy of no work—no food, but they would just snack before we came home. Nothing works!

DISCUSSION

In many families, some members take life easy, getting a great deal of service from other members, who work like slaves. Such a situation is unfair not only to those who work but to those who shirk. Part of the obligation of parents is to train their children to cooperate with the members of their group—to carry their share of the effort necessary for the group to function.

Before going further, let us make clear what we mean by "chores." Making one's bed is not a chore, nor is cleaning up one's room. Homework and putting away one's toys *are not chores!* A chore is a recurring activity that serves the whole family. If a child wipes up milk he has spilled on the floor, he is not performing a chore—he is only cleaning up his own mess. But if a child regularly puts milk in a dish for the family cat, this is a chore, since the cat is the family pet and someone in the family has to feed the animal. A chore benefits everyone—taking out the garbage, cooking meals, washing the dishes, driving the car to the store, buying the groceries, taking in the mail, and so forth.

Chores are not paid for. One does chores simply because one belongs to the family; it is fair to contribute to the general good since one obtains the benefits of the work of other members. There should be no connection between allowances and chores. A child should get his allowance whether or not he does chores, and he should do his chores whether or not he gets an allowance.

In a loving family in which good relations exist, use of the method we call *logical consequences* is not likely to be necessary with regard to chores. Discussions in the family council should settle readily the question of who is to do what, and the children should be quite willing to do their parts.

SOLUTION

The family should discuss the necessity and fairness of sharing the chores. It should be pointed out that Father goes to work for all and that Mother cooks, cleans, and shops for all. There should be discussion of how much time and effort each of the children should put in. Decisions on this point should be based on such factors as the child's age and his other activities, including school, baseball practice, piano practice, etc. A general formula such as this may be acceptable: to require chores at three or four and at that age to expect about five minutes a day; at six, ten minutes; at seven, fifteen; and so on up to age thirteen, when the time could be about an hour a day.

For nonperformance, the method of logical consequences should be followed:

(1) No one else should do the chore, so that it remains undone; (2) the person who wants to eat or sleep must first do his chore; (3) in extreme situations, a work stoppage on the part of the parents may be advisable (this should rarely be done).

Parents should not remind or nag.

SOLUTION APPLIED TO THE VERNON FAMILY

The counselor suggested a *parental strike* and told Mr. and Mrs. Vernon how to do it. Here is how it worked:

The parents did not do any shopping for several days but made no mention of this to the children. The family's supply of milk, bread, cereals, cookies, and other easily consumed foods diminished rapidly. Then one night the parents called a family meeting. Their kids paid attention to them because of their unusual gravity.

"You kids don't cooperate with us; you don't help out. Well, from now on we're not going to cooperate with you—not until you cooperate with us. Until then we won't cook for you, or make your beds, or do anything else for you."

The kids began to cheer, giggle, poke each other, and laugh. It was the biggest joke. Whoopee!

And so began the strike.

The following morning the parents left the house to have breakfast elsewhere. When they came home that night and saw no chores done, they turned around and went out to dinner, then to a movie. At about ten o'clock they came home, and the kids were watching television. Ordinarily the parents would have had a fit, demanding that the kids go to bed, brush their teeth, say their prayers, etc.; but instead the parents now just went to bed. And the next day they went through practically the same procedure. On Saturday, Mother did only her own and her husband's laundry, and then the two took off for the beach.

Except for the parents' bedroom and bathroom, which they kept spotless, the house was becoming more and more littered. When they noticed that the family dog wasn't getting fed, they took him away and left him with friends. The garbage from cans that the kids had opened was overflowing.

As recommended, Mr. and Mrs. Vernon had informed their neighbors, friends, and family of their parental strike and asked them not to feed the children; the couple also had asked the neighborhood grocer not to give them food. The two continued to spend as much time as possible away from home, eating their meals out and visiting friends frequently. They were not impolite to their children but simply maintained toward them a strict do-nothing policy. This state of affairs dragged on for six days.

On the evening of the seventh day, when Mr. and Mrs. Vernon came home to check on things, ready to go out for dinner together again if chores were not done, they found the kids lined up ready to discuss matters. The parents sat down with them. The problem was food. The conversation went somewhat as follows:

Son 1: We get nothing to eat.

Father: There is food in the house.

Son 1: You have to provide us with food we like.

Father: Who says so?

Son 2: It's the law.

Father: Then call the police and have us arrested.

Son 1: You ought to provide good food for us, not just canned food.

Father: You ought to do chores. We told you that if you cooperate with us, we'll cooperate with you.

Son 3: I want my dog back.

Father: If you had fed him, you would have him.

Son 4: I'm hungry. I want hamburgers.

Mother: I'm willing to cook but only if you kids cooperate with us.

Son 1: I'll cooperate.

Father: What do you mean?

Son 1: I'll do my chores.

Father: How about you others?

(All kids except Henry, age ten, agree to do their chores.)

Father: It isn't good enough. All of you have to agree. (Parents leave the house.)

Two days later, when the parents came home, the house was in good order: the huge pile of dishes had been washed, the garbage taken out, and almost everything was done except for certain chores that had been assigned to Henry, including raking leaves in the yard and sweeping the porch. As the parents looked around, the children followed them, a ragtag, dirty group.

Son 1: Well, we did our chores. Will you now feed us right?

Father: Only when *all* the chores are done.

Son 1: Only Henry didn't do his chores.

Father: Only when *all* the chores are done!

Son 2: It isn't fair. Why don't you feed us and not him?

Father: We'll cooperate with you when *all* of you cooperate with us.

Son 1: Henry, you jerk, we're going to kill you if you don't pitch in and do your work. (Henry runs out of house.)

Father: When *all* the chores are done and when *all* you kids agree to cooperate, we'll cooperate with you. (The children look disconsolate. Gone is their rowdiness. The parents leave again.)

On the next day, the ninth day of the parental strike, the parents found the whole house, inside and out, in spic-and-span order. Once again all five kids were present and another discussion ensued.

Son 1: Everything is O.K. now. Our rooms are clean. All the chores are done. Now will you stay home like you are supposed to?

Father: We will only if you all agree to cooperate the way you are supposed to.

Son 1: It's just him (pointing to Henry) who won't cooperate. We had to do his chores for him.

Father: I told you yesterday, and I'll tell you again, unless all of you kids agree to do your chores, and do them, we aren't going to do ours.

Son 2: Why should we be punished for Henry?

Father: Mother and I are treating all you kids alike. We are not going to deal with you individually. We found that when we tried to talk to one of you, or to discipline one of you, the rest of you began to act up.

Mother: Only when *all* of you agree will we agree to do our part.

Two days later—eleven days after the parental strike had started —almost the same scene was repeated.

The kids were wearing dirty clothes and smelled bad.

Son 1: Aren't you coming back home, like you used to do?

Father: If you kids aren't cooperative, we aren't going to play your game.

Son 1: We all agree to cooperate.

Father: Everyone? (All nod.) Well, then, since you all agree to cooperate—who will go with me to the store for shopping, to push the wagon? Mother will start the wash. (All the kids volunteer to go along with Dad, and he rolls out with five kids in the car, all of them happy.)

FURTHER EXAMPLES

Dade had agreed at a family council to take out the garbage. According to the rules for assigning chores, the parents had seen to it that all necessary elements were clearly understood:

Who—Dade
What—Take out garbage
Where—From kitchen to the trash can
When—By bedtime
How—Without spilling anything
Why—Fair for him to do some of the family work

The item most frequently overlooked is *When*. We strongly recommend that all *When*s be established in terms of "by such and such time"—and that this time be either just before a meal or just before bedtime.

Dade remembered the first and second nights, but the third night he forgot. Before going to bed, his mother checked under the sink and, sure enough, there was the garbage. She started to take it out, but her husband stopped her.

"Better leave it there."

"Insects will come."

"Spray it with bug killer."

Mother did just that, and left the garbage. The next day the can was overfull, and Mother had to put the sack with garbage on the floor. That night Dade remembered and, when he looked under the sink, saw that there was garbage all around. "Gee, I forgot," he said. "Well, just make sure you clean up the floor nicely," his mother said. He remembered for four more days, and then forgot for three. Mother kept using bug spray rather than saying anything, but finally she told her husband, "We just have to tell him. He sees nothing."

"Yes. I'll talk with him."

A few minutes later, Father had a talk with his son.

"Here's the story, Dade," Father said. "We know that people forget things from time to time, and we wonder what we can do about helping you to do your chore about the garbage."

"Oh, darn it—I forgot about it again. I'll take it away right now," the boy said hurriedly.

"Well, let's wait a bit. What I'm wondering is how can we help you to remember? First, maybe you don't want to take out garbage. What do you think? Maybe you want a different chore."

Dade considered. "No," he said finally. "That's all right."

"Do you want to remember?"

"Yes."

"We'll remind you then if you forget. Is that O.K.?"

"Sure. O.K."

"But it will help you most to remember if, when you forget, we remind you at inconvenient times, such as while you're watching television or are about to eat, or while you're playing, or even while you're asleep. How about that?"

"Huh?"

"The best way for you to learn to remember is for us to remind you at times that are unpleasant for you. So if you really want to remember, you have to give us permission to wake you up, or call you any time we want."

"Oh, O.K. I'll try to remember."

After this discussion, Dade remembered to do his chores for several weeks, but one night he forgot. Father woke Dade. Apparently in a state of dazed confusion, the boy took out the garbage.

"He looks as if he doesn't know what he's doing," Mother said. "It was useless to get him up."

"Nonsense," said Father. "I bet he won't forget tomorrow."

And Dade did not forget again, not, at least, for several months. The logical consequence, agreed to by Dade—that he be waked up if he forgot his chore—worked even though he seemed to be in a daze.

Nick wanted a dog badly. Father didn't like pets but finally agreed to get one only after Nick solemnly promised to take care of him. Nick promised to feed him, make sure he had water at all times, brush and comb his coat weekly, change a flea collar every three months, and pick up his droppings from the enclosed yard. Father was doubtful that Nick, who was ten years old, would keep his end of the contract, and he had the boy write a list of what he was to do and when he would do it. Nick was ecstatic and he kept meticulously to his agreement for exactly eight days. Then Mother noted that there was no water in the dog's pan. She reported Nick's misattention to Father. The parents had a conference with Nick. All he would say for himself was that he "forgot." Father suggested that if Nick couldn't take care of the dog, perhaps the family should sell it. Nick became quite upset and promised strongly to "remember" in the future. However, a week later, another conference was held because again Nick had "forgotten."

Mother came up with a suggestion acceptable to all: Nick was not to eat until he had done everything he had promised to do for the dog. Nick readily agreed to this, and this procedure solved the problem. The parents would wait until Nick was seated and just about to eat, and then they would ask him whether Pluto had been cared for. If he had not, Nick would jump up and attend to his chores. But for Nick to "forget" and have to leave the table became a very rare occurrence indeed.

SUMMARY

It is right for every member of a family to contribute to the family well-being. The size of this contribution is best determined by unanimous agreement among all the family members, including the contributor—all should agree that the arrangement is *fair*. For one member to do less than his "fair share" of family chores is morally wrong. It is equally wrong for a family member to do *more* than his share of those chores—no member should be, in effect, the others' servant.

Chores should be treated as a kind of contract: in return for the benefits of a family membership—shelter, food, clothing, allowances, etc.—a child should contribute through chores. In working out a list of chores, the questions *who, what, where, when, how,* and *why* should be discussed and answered by unanimous agreement. Perhaps the most important, as a practical matter, is *when*. Parents and child should also discuss and reach agreement on what is to be done if the child "forgets" to do the chore. Our suggestion is logical consequences affecting eating and sleeping: one doesn't eat until one does one's chores; one doesn't sleep until one does one's chores. But there must be free agreement on the part of the child to accept the consequence—otherwise it would be punishment.

The method of logical consequences for chores usually does not work with rebellious teen-agers but usually works quite well indeed with sub-teen-agers.

16 | *Clutter–Messiness*

Mrs. Rosenberg looked at the clock: five thirty-five. She then looked around her living room. A mess! Books, papers, toys strewn all around. Playing under the table were Tom and Tod, seven and eight. "Now hurry and clean up. Put all your things away. Dad will be home soon and you know he doesn't like to see things messy." Then she heard the hiss of boiling water overrunning the kettle and she ran to the kitchen. A minute later, Mother shouted, *"Did you put your things away?"* Her shrill voice energized them to get up and look around. Tod picked up a special toy, took it to his room, and tossed it on his bed, where a dozen other items already lay. The floor of his room was littered with toys and other paraphernalia dear to the hearts of children. Mother yelled again, and Tom picked up an item belonging to Tod. When Tod saw Tom with one of his toys, they got into a fight. At this point Father came home. When he saw the littered kitchen and living room, he blew up. "How is it that every time I come home the place looks like a pigpen?" he asked as his wife came to greet him. Her nerves snapped. "I wish you were here to do better!" she said as she flounced off.

Father set his teeth and didn't reply. He went to the TV and turned it off. The kids looked up in surprise. "Come on, scouts," Father said with forced gaiety. "It'll be time to eat soon. Let's clean up." Reluctantly, they began to pick up their things, with Father helping them. How long will it be before they learn to take care of their things and be reasonably neat? Father thought.

DISCUSSION

About neatness, two kinds of people make others uncomfortable: the compulsive neatniks and the compulsive slopniks. Some people get upset if anything is out of place; others just don't seem to care and leave a trail of misplaced objects behind them. Sloppiness, fighting, and "laziness" are the big three of family conflicts. Most children are not neat. (Indeed, a very neat child is probably not really happy—he may be trying to act overly good.)

How should parents train children to be reasonably neat and orderly?

SOLUTION

As is usual when we use a new technique with children, we should discuss it with them beforehand: what we expect from them and why, and what we will do if they do not comply with the rules. They should not only understand the new approach but should agree to its adoption. Communication can be effective only if it occurs in a low voice, when all are really listening. For this reason, the family council (see Chapter 33) is the best place for introducing changes. But the parents must not suggest a new procedure unless they have thought it through and are determined to follow it with calm, firm, undeviating consistency.

So let us now assume that the parents are tired of a sloppy house —they want to teach their children general habits of neatness and are willing to put in the necessary time and effort.

1. The parents should decide which areas are the children's to keep as they wish, which areas belong to the whole family, and which areas are for the parents alone. Separate rules can be made for each of the three areas. We recommend these general rules: (1) *You can do what you want in your own room;* (2) *you*

cannot ever mess up our room; and (3) *you can mess up the living room, kitchen, and yard; but if you do, you must clean them periodically.*

2. The next step should be one whose importance has already been stressed: the parents should discuss the new regime thoroughly with the children and get their agreement to it, including the rules for enforcing it (logical consequences).

3. If a child should "forget," he is to be reminded to clean up.

4. Reminding will be done at times convenient for the parent but inconvenient for the child, such as before a meal or late at night.

5. The child does not have to clean up when reminded. However, the parent may continue reminding and does not have to do anything for the child (such as feed him) until he does what he agreed to do.

Once the children are neat, parents must be very careful to deal promptly with occasional violations: if these are not dealt with immediately, things may slip back into the old situation. Keep in mind that children usually accept new rulings only after some initial resistance and that, after a period of cooperation, they often try again to test the parents—the second offensive. This second offensive calls for strong-minded parents who will refuse to become discouraged and will stick faithfully to the new procedures. There may even be a third offensive.

APPLICATION TO TOM AND TOD

The parents called in their boys for a discussion, after having themselves decided what they wanted to do to handle the problem of clutter in the house.

Father: Mother and I have been talking about keeping the house neat. We want you to learn how to put your things away. We have been doing a lot of yelling. From now on, we're not going to do it anymore.

Mother: And we're not going to punish you.

Tom: Hooray.

Tod: Good.

Father: So from now on we'll expect you to clean up before you come to eat.

Tom: What do you mean?

Father: You two can keep your own room the way you want. But the kitchen, the bathrooms, the living room, and the porch have to be cleared of all toys and books. And until they are cleaned up, Mother will not feed you.

Tom: Isn't that punishment?

Tod: Yeah, not letting little kids eat.

Mother: I want you to eat. You know that. But you will not be fed until you put your things away. That isn't punishment. It's to help you remember to straighten things up.

Father: What's more, at night, before you go to bed, you had better check to make sure you've put everything away because if you haven't, I'll remind you to do it.

Tom: Suppose I'm asleep.

Father: Then I'll wake you up. I want you two to learn to cooperate with us.

Tom: All right. I'll put things away.

Tod: Tom makes the biggest mess of all.

Father: Another thing: I don't want anything to happen like what happened yesterday with that toy car.

Mother: What was that?

Father: I asked the kids to put that car away. It was right in the middle of the kitchen floor, where someone could step on it and maybe slip and get hurt. Tom said it wasn't his, that he had given it to Tod; and Tod said it belonged to Tom. So *I* had to put it away: I threw it in the garbage can. And then Tod went to get it.

Tom: See—it was his!

Tod: *Now* it *is* mine. You said it wasn't yours.

Father: Well, from now on, to stop squabbling like that, *neither one* of you will eat until *everything* is cleared up.

Tom: That isn't fair. Suppose it's *his* stuff?

Father: I don't care. We don't want to argue about whose stuff it is or who put it there. If the place is cluttered by either of you, neither of you eats until it's cleaned up. And the two of you can settle between yourselves who left what. The same thing at night. If I see anything around, I'll wake up both of you if necessary and keep on doing it until things are put away. Do you both understand?

Tom: Yes. But I still think it's not fair.

Father: All right, what *is* fair?

Tom: Find out who did it. Don't punish me if Tod left out stuff.

Father: But suppose you said Tod left it and he said you left it —what should we do?

Tom: Then let Tod and me settle it.

Father: What do you say to that, Tod?

Tod: Yes, that's all right.

Mother: It seems all right to me too. If the children can agree who left what around and each one puts back everything he's responsible for, fine; if not, then they don't eat until they settle matters between themselves.

Father: All right, but if you can't agree, we won't settle it for you. For instance, suppose I go into the kitchen after both of you are in bed and I find one of your things on the floor. What should I do?

Tom: Wake up the one who left it.

Father: Suppose it's a book and I don't know whose book it is?

Tod: Oh, what's a book in the kitchen? Do we have to have everything just so neat?

Mother: All day long I'm putting things away. I'm embarrassed when people come because I have to run around and put your things away.

Tod: Why don't you do what Mrs. Madden does? She just throws everything in a box and the kids have to dig their things out.

Mother: I want you to become responsible. Why should I pick up after you? That isn't fair to me.

Tom: Oh, all right. I don't know why you want to make such a big fuss about it.

Mother: I just want you two to be fair to me. I want you to learn to be cooperative. Do we all understand one another?

Both children nodded, and thus the family had achieved agreement on principles and procedures.

When Father came home next evening, he was pleased to see that the living room was neat. At dinnertime the kids came to the table and sat down to eat. They were reaching for the food when Mother spoke.

Mother: You can eat when you put everything away.

Tom: What?

Tod: What?

Mother: When you put everything away, you can eat.

Tom: What's out of place?

Mother: It's up to you to find out. I just checked and I found something out of place in the bathroom.

Tom got up, went into the bathroom, and came back.

Tom: It's Tod's boat.

He sat down. Both kids looked at each other, each determined to eat, each determined to make an issue of that boat.

Mother fed Father and herself. The kids looked on. Finally, Tod got up and looked in the bathroom.

Tod: It *is* my boat, but Tom had it last and he left it on the floor of the bathroom. But anyhow, I just put it away.

Mother (smiling): O.K. Let's all eat now.

At bedtime, the kids said good night, washed up, and went to bed. Mother noted a toy badge and a child's book on the floor in the living room, under a chair. She went to the kids' bedroom door and knocked.

"What is it?" Tom asked.

"There's something in the living room," she said, and walked away.

Neither kid got up.

Fifteen minutes later, she again knocked on the door. No answer. She knocked louder until finally Tom, sleepily, asked what it was all about.

Instead of answering, she walked away.

"Why didn't you tell them why you woke them up?" Father asked.

"I've told them once and that's enough," Mother replied. "I intend not to let them sleep until these two things are returned, and I don't care how long it takes."

Fifteen minutes later, she banged on the door again. Tom came to the living room and looked around, his eyes glazed.

"Where is it?" he asked.

Neither parent answered.

"Well, won't you tell me?" he demanded, angry now.

The parents still did not answer.

He looked around, picked up the toy badge, and went back to bed, leaving the book under the chair.

Fifteen minutes later, Father knocked on the door. No answer. He pounded his palm loudly against the door until he heard the kids awakening. Then he walked away. Fifteen minutes later, back he went and pounded until he heard the kids ask what he wanted. He didn't answer. Back he went to look at television. Fifteen minutes later, he got up and was about to start pounding again—and then he noticed that the book had been picked up while he was looking at TV.

It took about ten days for the children to be trained. During that period both parents examined the house before each meal and before bedtime each night. By the end of the period, when it was time to eat or time to go to bed, both kids looked to see that every object for which they were responsible had been put in its proper place.

In this incident, a new element has been brought in, which we call "unitism"—treating children alike when only one of them is "guilty" but the parents can't know which one it is. While it may sound unfair not to let both children eat if one of them refuses to put away his things, we have found "unitism" is better than attempting to deal with each child separately. Let's see why:

Mother: Tod, when you put away your truck, you can eat.

Tod: Tom borrowed my truck and played with it. He took it without permission. You should tell *him* to put it away.

Mother: What do you say about that, Tom?

Tom: I *didn't* play with it. Tod and his friend Bruce were playing with it last!

Tod: That isn't true! I found the truck on the couch. Tom had used some Magic Markers on it. So Bruce and I cleaned it up.

Mother: Why didn't you return it after you cleaned it?

Tod: He should have returned it. He took it out of the room.

Tom: That's a lie! I found the truck on the couch. I think Tod put it there. I painted it just for fun.

Mother: You shouldn't have done that.

Tom: He should look after his things better.

. . . and on and on and on and on.

Applying "Unitism"

> Mother: Kids, you may eat when that truck is put away.
> Tod: Tom took it out of the bedroom.
> (Mother is silent.)
> Tom: I did not.
> (Mother is silent.)

And Mother remains silent and doesn't feed either of the kids until the truck is put away. She refused to get entangled in arguments on whose truck it is, who took it, who is responsible.

FURTHER EXAMPLES

Mrs. Mundy looked the counselor in the eye and said challengingly, "We have a problem that is absolutely unsolvable. We've tried *everything.*"

"What is the problem?"

"Dick, our eleven-year-old, and our two girls, ten and six, have one bathroom and we have another. He just will not pull up the seat when he urinates, and he wets the seat."

"What happens?"

"Well, if the girls see that the seat is wet, they come to me or to my husband and tell us. But sometimes they sit and get wet. And then we go after him."

"What happens?"

"Well, we ask him why he did it, and his reply always is 'I forgot.' And then we make him clean it."

"How long has this been going on?"

"Ever since he's been standing up."

"Have you tried any other method of teaching him?"

"Like I said, we've tried everything we could think of. We put a sign on the wall so that when he is standing up he has to see it. Once my husband glued a little rubber insect on the inside of the bowl so he could aim at it. And of course we tried spanking him. Once my husband even made him lick the toilet seat. Nothing works. The girls sometimes use our bathroom, and we're thinking of giving Dick the children's bathroom just for himself, but we don't think that would be right."

"So you feel you have tried everything and that nothing works —that nothing ever will work."

"Yes."

The counselor smiled and said, "I have a suggestion that may work. What is more, it will probably work after only one trial. What do you think of that?"

"Surgery?" the mother asked, smiling ruefully.

The counselor laughed. "No, nothing so drastic. But the question is whether you are willing to do exactly what I tell you."

"If it won't hurt him."

"Come now, Mother, do you think I want to hurt him?"

"What is it?"

"It's simple. Tell him that as soon as you find out that he has wet the toilet seat, you will ask him to clean it—"

"But that is what we *do*."

"—no matter where he is."

"What does that mean?"

"Just what I said."

"But I don't understand."

"You will. From now on, as soon as you learn he has wet the seat, no matter what the time may be, day or night, remind him gently to clean it."

"But suppose he isn't home. He leaves for school earlier than the girls."

"Then go wherever he is and remind him."

"But suppose he has gone to school?"

The counselor smiled. "Now, Mrs. Mundy, what do you think I am going to advise you to do?"

The mother thought and finally a smile came over her face too. "Do you mean reach him at school to remind him to come home to wipe it up?"

The counselor nodded.

"But what will that do to him?" she asked.

The counselor shrugged. "I don't know. I can't be sure. It's up to you whether or not you want to try it. I will say, though, that I think it quite likely that this will help him to stop this inconsiderate habit."

Mother shook her head. "I'll have to discuss this with my husband."

Several weeks later, the mother returned to the counselor and announced, "The problem is solved. Dick isn't doing it anymore."

"What happened?"

"Well, I discussed it with my husband and he said your idea made sense. We called in Dick, and I told him if he ever again wet the toilet seat we would get him wherever he was, whether he was playing, in the movies, visiting, in school, in church—wherever. He understood we meant it and, sure enough, we didn't have any complaints from the girls for about ten days—the longest period he had ever gone without wetting the seat. And then one morning the girls came to me saying, 'He did it again.' I checked; it was true. He had just left for school, so I finished my dishes and then went to the school. At the school office I asked the clerk if she would call Dick. She wanted to know why, but I wouldn't tell her. Then she had me talk to the vice principal, and I told him. He laughed, told me I was doing the right thing, and went after Dick. He came back, with Dick beside him, stiff and straight and white-faced. I walked with Dick to the car, saying nothing. In the car he exploded. I jumped out and looked away from the car while he had a temper tantrum like never before. He was screaming, yelling, biting his hand, punching around. I just waited until he calmed down. Then I got in the car. En route he said nothing. When we got home, he banged into the house, threw himself on the floor, and started another temper tantrum, yelling that he would never go to school again—that I had embarrassed him for life. I have learned enough now to handle temper tantrums, so I went into my bathroom and turned on the radio. Then Dick went into his room, slammed the door, and said he was never, never, never going back to that school. He stayed in his room from about nine o'clock until maybe eleven. I don't know what he was doing, but I didn't hear any music or anything. Finally, he came out, ready for battle. He began yelling at me, and I listened with a pleasant expression until finally he ran down. Then I said:

" 'Dick, all I want you to do is clean off the toilet seat.'

"We then had some more yells and screams and complaints, and then he went back into his room. He came out again about eleven-thirty. Again he started picking on me, but I didn't answer. Well, eventually he did clean it. I made some lunch for both of us, frankfurters, but said nothing to him about eating. He finally came into the kitchen and snatched the sausages and ate them in the living room. Around a quarter to one, when the lunch period at school was about over, with classes due to start at one, he asked me, 'Will you take me back to school?' 'Of course,' I told him. And I took him back. That was about two weeks ago, and we haven't had any complaints since then. Looks like there's a solution to everything."

"Do you feel that you harmed Dick by this procedure?"

"No, I don't. He simply experienced the logical consequences of his behavior. He had a severe lesson, but it was not punishment, and he had due warning. And if he ever wets the seat again, I'll remind him again wherever he is—and he knows it."

"What have *you* learned, Mrs. Mundy?"

"One thing is that punishment doesn't work. My husband had really walloped Dick several times, and we used to punish him in a lot of other ways. Once we made him stay in the bathroom for six hours without any books or anything. At another time my husband tied him to the toilet for hours. And I nagged, nagged, and nagged Dick, and that didn't work. I was really convinced he was crazy or something. When you suggested what you did, it seemed wrong to me at first but now it seems logical. Anyway, it stopped his behavior. And he doesn't seem upset. We no longer have to yell at him or hit him or anything. The girls are happier. And I think *he* is happier too."

A mother at a Family Education Center said that her husband and their four children, twelve, nine, six, and three, were inconsiderate and never put anything away.* They didn't put dirty clothes in the hampers, they didn't hang up their clothes, they left everything everywhere—and the house was a mess. A social worker who made a home visit reported that the house was filthy and stank. The mother talked, talked, talked—but no one in the family lis-

---

* This incident, in an expanded form, was reported in *The Individual Psychologist,* 7 (1970): 47–51.

tened to her. She felt desperate. Her husband was physically handicapped and was no help with the children.

A plan was suggested to the mother, to be put into effect only if her husband agreed. He did so. And so—

One night, after supper, Mother asked the children which they would prefer: (*a*) that she continue nagging them to put their things away or (*b*) that she start acting like the rest of the family, never tidying up but just letting things lie or kicking them out of sight, etc. They liked plan *b*.

So Mother stopped her nagging and let everything pile up. She kept her own room clean. Within a week, she reported, things everywhere in the house were piled high, and the children had no clean clothes. This didn't seem to bother them at all. But Mother was quite upset: what would the teachers think if the kids came in smelling and wearing dirty clothes? The counselor advised Mother to continue the program. A week later, when she reported again, Mother was practically desperate. The kids now were really filthy, and the house was like a junkshop. She was advised to continue in her new way without deviation.

At this point her children were interviewed. They were dirty but happy and smiling and didn't think that there was any real problem.

Three weeks later, when seen again by the counselor, Mother was even more upset. Some of the children were complaining that they wanted new clothes—but the hamper was empty. She reported that one child, her nine-year-old daughter, was starting to hang up some of her things. Mother had even complimented the girl. "Stop it," Mother was told. "No compliment should be paid to a child for doing what she is supposed to do." Mother was asked to continue in the same way—to let the situation get worse.

Four weeks after the initial conference, Mother came back again and informed us that on the prior Saturday the four kids had gone on a cleaning bee: they had kept the washing machine going for almost twelve hours straight, and they had put everything away. For the first time in many years, the house was neat.

And she reported something else: the three younger children had been bed-wetters. She had never mentioned this to the counselor because she was ashamed to say it. After first being counseled, she had decided, on her own but in harmony with the advice the counselor had given her, not to do any more cleaning up after them—to let them drown, so to speak, in their own urine. She hadn't done their sheets for four weeks. The middle two children had stopped wetting the bed, and the three-year-old was skipping every once in a while! Thus she had hit upon the right way to stop the bed-wetting (see Chapter 29). She had helped the children conquer this problem by her refusal to continue being their servant.

Her previous efforts to change the kids by helping them and nagging them had been useless, but her new procedure of giving them responsibility had worked. Within a matter of weeks, the family had become reasonably happy, with a house that was relatively neat and three younger children who no longer wet the bed.

SUMMARY

Talk the problem over with your children, come to an agreement with them, and then *never again discuss the matter*—just carry out the agreed procedure without anger. Keep to that procedure without fail.

We have found that the two methods suggested here work well: in one, food and sleep are tied to neatness; in the other, things are allowed to go to pot. Whether you adopt one or the other, your children will resist and may try to outwait you. Before trying either method, resolve that you will be inflexible: no food or no sleep until things have been put away; or, if the second method has been chosen, let things go until the kids take responsibility.

It goes without saying that parents who want their kids to be neat should themselves be good examples.

17 | *Own Room*

"Do you remember the lecture you gave Harold last week about keeping his room clean?" Mrs. James asked her husband. "Well, come and see it."

In the large, well-lit room was a desk, two chests of drawers, and a bunk bed. A chair, a bookcase, and a large toy chest completed the furnishings. On the top bunk were various items of clothing that Mrs. James had washed and pressed. On the desk, chair, and floor were soiled clothing: socks, undershirts, a pair of pants, a jacket, and a coat. Piled on top of the desk were papers, magazines, and books. The floor was littered with toys, sports equipment, and other possessions dear to eleven-year-old boys.

"Looks like a junkshop," Father said. "How can we teach that boy to be neat? We've tried everything."

"I'm ashamed to let anyone see this room. It really is a disgrace," Mrs. James said.

"I suppose we just have to keep after him," said her husband.

"But we've been after him for years, telling him to clean up, refusing to give him his allowance if it wasn't clean, calling him in from play to clean it up, telling him he's inconsiderate. I feel we've failed completely. How on earth can we ever get him to be neat?"

"Maybe there is no way," Father stated. "Maybe boys are just naturally sloppy."

DISCUSSION

Criticizing, advising, preaching, bribing, withdrawing privileges, taking away allowances, and other forms of reward and punishment usually work—but not for long. Yet there is a solution. We have seen hundreds of children learn to keep their rooms neat and tidy. Unfortunately, it is a solution that usually takes a long time. Most of the procedures that we suggest in this book for particular problems work satisfactorily within a week or so; the procedure we are about to explain can take up to a year. But remember: it usually works.

SOLUTION

The parents agree with the child that he has a right to keep his own quarters just as he wishes—that his room is *his* business. In effect, they make a contract with him as follows: "We will supply the room for you if you promise to take care of it one hundred percent. We'll not pick on you for its condition. You are free to keep it just as you wish. It is *your* place."

The parents' hope is that the room will soon get so untidy and so uncomfortable that the child will realize, on his own, the necessity for cleaning and making it orderly. They should realize that some children may never become as neat as parents would like them to be.

One of the great advantages of this procedure is that the parents no longer get angry about the room. And they should not let themselves become upset by the opinions of members of the family or visitors.

It is essential for the parents to disregard the room once the contract is made. They must act as if the room doesn't exist, and say nothing about it. If cockroaches, mice, or other undesirable vermin come into it, they can disinfect the area outside the room. A mechanical door closer may be used to keep the child's door shut if the sight of the room is upsetting to the parents. However, they should not install this gadget unless they have the child's permission.

If the room is kept fairly neat from the beginning, be happy; but if it is kept completely dirty and disorganized, be even happier— your child will come to realize fully the value of cleanliness and order even sooner.

Is this method fair and feasible when two or more children share a room? Yes. The general principle to follow is this: *kids settle any problems about the room themselves.* It is a basic error for parents to try to enforce justice between children—to try to judge the fairness of their relationships with each other. We urge: *Don't.* The child who seems weakest is often strong enough to hold his own if given a chance. When parents intervene, the usual result is greater rather than less friction between the children.

Our method works best when applied strictly as we have outlined it. If that is not feasible, parents may, of course, make necessary modifications. However, they should be very careful not to introduce variations that weaken or dilute the method to such an extent that it cannot develop responsibility in the child. Here are some possible variations:

1. The child agrees that he will have his room in order at least one day a week, otherwise he cannot go out. On that day his room must stand inspection. The best day for this is Saturday. So the child keeps the room as he wishes six days a week, but on Saturday he cannot leave the house until the room is clean and neat.

This alternative is not as good as completely giving the child his room—the parents are taking some responsibility. And if they check closets and drawers there will almost certainly be arguments about whether things are properly or improperly stowed away.

2. The parents agree to help with a periodic cleanup. This may take place, say, once a month: beds are made, room is washed and vacuumed, etc.

We suggest that every fourth Saturday morning be agreed upon for the cleanup and that Mother work rather slowly but methodically. The child will then want to work quickly to get it over with and go out and play. The date should be written on a piece of paper kept in the child's room so that he will be reminded of the engagement. As the date approaches, he may begin to keep the room in better order so that he will not be kept in too long.

We caution that no nagging or complaining or advising be done. Let this cleanup period be a pleasant one. Mother should elicit directions from the child, saying, "Now, where do you want me to put this?" rather than "Please put your skates in the toy box!"

SOLUTION APPLIED TO HAROLD

"Harold, Father and I have been talking about your room," Mrs. James began.

"Oh, I'll keep it clean from now on," Harold began, expecting a lecture.

"No, we want to discuss something else," Mrs. James went on. "We want to give you the room."

"Huh?" said Harold suspiciously.

"If you agree to take complete charge of it, we will agree never to say a single word about it. It will be yours to do with as you wish."

"As a matter of fact, Harold," Father added, "you can keep it as neat or as dirty as you want, and we'll not say a word."

Harold looked at his parents. "You mean . . . you won't pick on me anymore?"

"Exactly. The room is yours, keep it just as you want. But you have to agree to take care of it. I'll no longer vacuum it or dust it or anything. As a matter of fact, Father and I will agree not even to enter your room without permission, unless there is some emergency. Now, will you accept the room?"

"OK. And I can keep it just as I want?"

"It will be your room. I'll show you how to make the bed and how to vacuum it," said Mother.

Father added, "There is just one thing I want to ask you to do."

"What's that?" asked Harold, his suspicions flaring.

"The one thing is that you keep your door closed so that if Mother and I happen to pass by we can't see how you keep it."

"I promise," said Harold.

"Good!" said Mother. "I think you are old enough to become responsible."

After that there was no more discussion about Harold's room. Once a week, when Harold was not in the house, the parents looked in his room.

First week. The room is immaculate. Everything is put away neatly. It looks like a room at West Point.

Second week. There are five or six items on the floor and about a dozen scattered elsewhere about the room.

Third week. There are now about a dozen items on the floor and two dozen scattered about. The bed has not been made since the end of the first week. The sheets are now a bit gray.

Fourth to sixth week. The bed linens have not been changed yet. There are about one hundred items on the floor: newspapers and books, clothing, toys, tools, pencils. There are many items cluttering the tops of the bureaus, desk, and bed. At the foot of the bed is a pile of dirty clothes. The top bunk is covered with clean clothing which Mother had originally deposited outside Harold's door.

Seventh to twelfth week. Bed still not made. The sheets are now dark gray. The pillowcase is almost black where Harold's hair hits it. The floor, bed, and desk are now about four inches deep in things: coats, shirts, shorts, socks, hats, toys. Mother wants to take a tranquilizer when she looks in the room.

Thirteenth week. Inexplicably the room is neat. Everything is in place. Linen has been changed. Parents, amazed, say nothing.

Thereafter, at the end of one week there might be nothing out of place, at the end of another there might be fifty items. The condition of the room varied—*but every two or three weeks it would be cleaned.* One day Mother heard Harold vacuuming the room, and a little later on she noticed he had some friends visiting him. She realized that he had finally learned the lesson. And from that point on, although the room wasn't always too presentable, it was at least usually fairly comfortable and neat.

FURTHER EXAMPLES

We will never forget one of our first cases. Mother was confined to a wheelchair. Father did all the cooking, washing, cleaning, and shopping. Their boys, eight and nine, did their chores reluctantly. The parents expected the children to clean their room, but it was a shambles. Father, in anger, stated that he had tried "everything" to get the kids to clean up. He had cried, telling them how hard he worked and how crippled their mother was. Then he had lost his temper and whipped them severely. He had taken them to the parish priest. Nothing worked. When we advised him that he should give the children the room and that they would eventually clean it, he stated emphatically· that this would not work—that he had tried this system. We asked how long he had tried it. "For several weeks," he replied sadly. "Not long enough," we told him. "You must try longer." "How much longer?" "For about ten more years," he was told.

Finally, both parents agreed to give this procedure a real try.

Periodically, they reported by telephone. The usual message went something like this: "I don't know how they can live in such dirt. My God, you should see the place. It's filthy. There's stuff in one corner piled three feet high. The room stinks. I don't know how long I can take it."

One afternoon Mother called. She cried hysterically that her children were fighting. "They really mean it this time. They're really battling. They're locked in their room and I can't get in it to stop them!"

"What is the fight all about?"

"I have no idea."

"Please call me when you know."

Next morning Father called.

He had looked in the children's room and, to his surprise, everything was in order, with nothing on the floor, the beds made, and the junk all put away. He and his wife looked at the room in wonder—and they noticed a chalk line across the floor. This line ran up the wall and continued across the ceiling, cutting the bedroom in two parts!

Later they discovered that the older boy had beaten the younger one because he had let another boy into the bedroom. This visitor had told other kids about the filthiness of the room, and all of them had made fun of the brothers because of it. After this battle they decided to divide the room, with each to clean up half.

We once visited a family we had counseled and, on coming in, were asked to look at their eight-year-old son's room. It was a typical disaster, with everything strewn around in complete disorder. Our hostess said, "I'm doing what you said. Isn't that room awful?" "Well, it sure looks messy. How do you feel about it?" we asked in return. "At first it drove me up the wall to see it, but now I have calmed down and I'm curious to learn how long it will take him to begin to clean it up. It has been more or less like this for the past month, and we started the program about two months ago. I'm beginning to think he will never clean it up."

We went on to meet some of the other guests and have dinner. When it was time to go home, our hostess once again suggested we look at the room. We wondered why she asked us. She opened the door to her son's room and we looked in. The room seemed in perfect order! "What happened?" we whispered. She whispered back, "See, on the top bunk? Jimmy has a new friend staying with him. About eight o'clock he asked me if this friend could stay overnight, and I said that he could. Between eight o'clock and nine-fifteen, when this boy arrived, Jimmy managed to clean that room. I would have thought that it would take him three hours to do it. I suppose all the stuff is just pushed out of sight into closets and drawers. But what really surprised me was to learn that he is even aware of the condition of the room!"

SUMMARY

As soon as he is old enough to be able to do it, the child should clean his room and make his bed. He will take pride in his own room if he is in charge of it.

Children are not naturally neat. However, if parents keep the rest of the house neat and clean and if they allow the child to experience the natural consequences of a messy room, he will eventually learn that living in a mess is unpleasant and unnecessary.

18 | *Money and Property*

THE PROBLEM

"Daddy, can I have a quarter?"

"What for?"

"Something I want."

"What?"

"A water pistol."

"A water pistol?"

"Yes."

"Why?"

"Alfred has one."

"Ask him to let you borrow his."

"He won't let me have it."

"Well, Walter, wait until he is through, then lend him something of yours."

"I want it *now*."

"Well, you can't have it now. Besides, I'm mad at you. You left my hammer out on the porch. Now it's rusty."

"I forgot."

"Well, you're not getting a water gun."

"Daddy, I *want* the water gun. Just give me a quarter!"

"Absolutely not!"

Conflicts about money and property are extremely common in families. The only problems more troublesome are disagreements about raising children.

SOLUTION

Here are some general rules:
1. All children who understand the concept of money should have money of their own which they may use without personal interference.
2. Parents should not get involved in money deals with their children.
3. Children should not be made to beg for money. Allowances should be a right and not a privilege.
4. Property or money should not be used for reward or punishment.
5. Children should be given opportunities to earn money at fair rates.
6. Children should be taught to respect other people's property. Children receive money in four forms: *gifts* (Grandmother sends five dollars to Billy for his birthday); *expense money* (money given to Harvey to pay for school lunch); *spending money* (Ted gets a sum with which to purchase snacks, candy, drinks, toys); and *earned money* (Frank gets a dime for filling a book with trading stamps, or a quarter for shining his father's shoes).

In all cases, whether the amount be ten cents or a thousand dollars, the money belongs to the child, and he should have the absolute right to buy what he wishes with it—or even to give it away. If a six-year-old wants to buy a bicycle that he cannot yet use with a hundred-dollar gift from a doting uncle, he has the right to do so. Children must be permitted to make mistakes, for that is the best way for them to learn—allowing them to make mistakes and to learn therefrom is the essence of the child-training method called *natural consequences.* Parents do have the obligation to explain to the child their own attitudes about money and to give him a reasonable amount of advice; but the child's money is *his* money, and no one else has the right to insist that he use it in a certain way.

When it comes to "borrowing" things, parents have a right to demand that their own things be respected. They should discuss rules, regulations, and consequences with the child.

1. Dangerous things such as weapons or power tools should be hidden, locked up, or made inoperable. A parent who leaves keys in his car is asking for trouble and possibly someone's death. So is a parent who leaves a loaded gun in the house—even an unloaded one if bullets for it can be reached by a child. A power saw should be made inoperable and kept out of a young child's reach. Dangerous drugs should be kept inaccessible to children, under lock and key.

2. Parents and child should enter an agreement that if he is permitted to handle equipment, tools, or other items for his own use and "forgets" to return them to their proper places, then the parents may remind him to return them. Reminding is most effective if done at a time *inconvenient for the child.* The child who uses a saw and leaves it out on the grass should not be asked to return it when he comes into the house but later when he is looking at television or just as he is about to get his first bite of dinner or just as he is about to climb into bed or even after he has fallen asleep (see Chapter 16). These "reminders" are exactly that: they are not orders—they must always be done in a gentle manner. But if the reminder is not heeded, it is repeated periodically until it *is* heeded.

3. If a child misuses equipment, then the parent has the right to make that equipment "off limits" for a definite period (this should usually be short).

4. If a piece of equipment is misused and it is impossible to determine which child misused it, it can be made off limits to all children in the family—innocent and guilty alike (this is an application of *unitism,* which is discussed in Chapter 16).

5. If one child uses another's equipment, toys, or other property and a ruckus ensues, we recommend that parents keep out of it— that they do not try to arbitrate. Solutions to such problems can come (*a*) through the family council (see Chapter 33), in which the children can settle the issue with the help of the parents, or (*b*) through letting the kids settle these issues between themselves.

APPLICATION TO THE WATER PISTOL INCIDENT

There are two problems: (1) the child's begging for money and

(2) the child's having used tools he did not return. Let us show how the two problems can be settled through the family council:

Father: Walter asked yesterday for a quarter to buy a water pistol.

Walter: Alfred has one. Why can't I have one too?

Mother: Alfred used the money that Grandma sent him.

Walter: Well, she didn't send me any.

Mother: It was his birthday and she sent him a dollar. He asked me to get him the gun, and I did. When your birthday comes, you can buy what you want with money Grandma sends you.

Walter: But I want a water gun now. We can play together.

Mother (to Father): I think we ought to give both Walter and Alfred some spending money that they can use for whatever they want.

Father: Shouldn't they earn their money?

Mother: I would think so except that, being only four and six, they are too young. I think it would be nice if they had some money regularly.

Father: O.K. How much would you boys want?

Alfred: I don't know.

Walter: A dollar.

Father: A dollar! What would you do with so much money?

Walter: Spend it.

Father: A dollar a day? A dollar a week?

Walter: I don't know.

Mother: I asked some of the other mothers around here, and they give their kids about a quarter a week.

Walter: I'm bigger than Alfred, and I should get more.

Mother: How about a quarter for Alfred and thirty cents for you?

Walter: O.K.

Alfred: How many dimes in a quarter?

Mother: Two dimes and one nickel.

Alfred: Can I have it now?

Father: Yes, if we decide to do it.

Alfred: How much is thirty cents?

Father: It's a quarter and a nickel—or three dimes. So we'll give Alfred a quarter every week and Walter thirty cents. It will be your money, and you can spend it how you want. Payday will be every Saturday morning. O.K?

Walter and Alfred: O.K.

Mother: Now, there is something else I want to bring up, and that has to do with borrowing things and not putting them away. Somebody took my good scissors yesterday, the ones I use for cutting material when I'm sewing. A lot of paper was all around the floor, and my scissors were on the floor too. From now on, I don't want you to use my good scissors. You have your own scissors, and you should use them.

Walter: It wasn't me.

Father: The same with my tools. If you use them, please put them away. You used my hammer last week, and you left it out on the porch and it got all rusty.

Walter: Mother called me in to lunch.

Father: Next time you use my tools and you don't put them back, I'll just ask you to return them. All right? Will you do that —just put them back?

Walter: Yes.

Father: If you don't put things back, we'll have to remind you.

Boys: O.K.

FURTHER EXAMPLES

The Cater family—parents and four children, two to six—were being counseled regarding family problems. On their third visit they reported that at their family council they established an allowance of seventeen cents a week per child. The money was distributed during the meeting, and the children put their money in small purses which they then hung on four hooks in a hallway. Grocery shopping was done on Saturday afternoon as a family outing, and each child took his purse along. "But why seventeen cents?" asked the counselor. Mother replied, "That gives each a dime, a nickel, and two pennies; they could spend each amount separately or combined." She added, "They all bought candy, so Father and I bought a candy bar too; we got home and had a party, eating the candy. But that was our only candy for that whole week." "Sounds good," said the counselor.

Mr. Hilliard, an accountant, had an office in his house, which was near a beach. He kept his typewriter covered because the damp air was bad for it. He had two children, Laura and Benny, eleven and twelve. One day Benny asked whether he could use the typewriter. The father said to both kids:

"I don't mind your using my typewriter if you will do two things. One: straighten up after you use the machine—don't leave any papers around; two: put the cover back on. If I find one of you has failed to do these things, that person can't use the typewriter anymore until I give permission."

Both kids agreed, and everything went well for about a week. One day Father found the typewriter cover on the floor. He asked the children, but each denied having used the typewriter. Father found in a wastebasket a sheet with typing that made him suspect it was Benny who had used the machine. Besides, Laura's outcries of outraged innocence were much stronger than Benny's. However, instead of accusing Benny and depriving him of the typewriter, Mr. Hilliard deprived *both children* of it for a week.

"But," cried angry Laura, "he used it, not I. Why can't I use it now?"

"I did *not* use the typewriter," Benny stated with unconvincing force.

"I don't care who it was," said Father, "and I am not going to try to find out. It is my typewriter, and I will not let either of you use it for the rest of the week. Is that understood?"

Several days later, Benny "confessed" he was the guilty one. Father again had a conference with the children, and this time only Benny was not to use the machine. But if Benny had not made this confession, Father's first ruling would have stood. Father was applying *unitism*. Unitism must be distinguished from mass punishment. If the father had, say, spanked both children or deprived both of dessert or fined both, that would have been punishment— and it would have been unfair. But to protect his property by saying, "Since I don't know who did it, I won't let either of you use my machine," is perfectly fair, even if an innocent child is deprived of a privilege.

Paul, nine, received a five-hundred-dollar inheritance and asked if with it he could buy anything he wanted. His father and mother told him that it was his money and that he could buy anything he wanted within reason. What did he want?

A motorcycle!

The parents argued against it but to no avail. Finally, after considerable discussion, they agreed to let him buy a motorcycle. Saturday morning, they went with their son to a motorcycle dealer, who, when he saw the child, said he was too young. The boy insisted, and the dealer gave him a wild test ride. A badly frightened boy got off the machine—and changed his mind. He decided he wanted a ten-speed bicycle, and the family went home with one.

Had the boy succeeded in purchasing a motorcycle, the parents would then have taken him to the police station to have him try to get a license, knowing full well that none would be issued to him.

Instead of fighting with the boy, the parents were wise enough to appear to give in—to let the child learn by experience. If the boy *had* succeeded in buying a motorcycle, it would have been a constant reminder to him of his bullheadedness, because he could not ride it until he was older.

"Hey, Dad, can I have an electric guitar?" asked Mike, fourteen.

Later that night, Mike's parents discussed his request at length. Next day, they priced the outfit Mike wanted—it cost over five hundred dollars. That night they had a talk with Mike.

"About the guitar—we found that it costs over five hundred dollars."

"I know it."

"We asked a music teacher and he thinks you ought to first learn to play a regular guitar, and after you know how, we can discuss whether we should buy such an expensive instrument."

"I don't want to learn on a regular guitar. I want an electric one."

The matter was dropped at this point.

The parents had another discussion without Mike's presence.

"He'll be intrigued with the guitar for a week, and then he won't play it and we'll be stuck with a five-hundred-dollar gadget," Father said.

"Well, we can't condemn him in advance," Mother replied.

The next day, after the parents had made further inquiries, they had another talk with Mike.

"Mike, if you'll make the down payment on the guitar, we'll pay the rest of it."

"Huh?"

"Do you want the guitar?"

"I told you I did."

"Well, here's what we propose: you make the down payment on the guitar; there'll be monthly payments after that—we'll pay those."

"What does that mean?"

"If we buy it on the installment plan, it'll cost not five hundred but six hundred. You make the down payment—the first eighty dollars. Then we will pay all of the remaining five hundred and twenty. I'll write it out for you."

	Mike	*Parents*	*Total*
Down payment	$80		
Payments		$520	
Total	$80	$520	$600

"We'll pay more than six times what you pay, but the guitar will be yours."

"You know I don't have any money."

"Oh—don't you have some savings?"

"Just what's in the bank. Twenty-five dollars from my Christmas money."

"Well, if you'll work and earn another fifty-five dollars, that will make eighty dollars."

"It'll take me a year to earn that much."

"No. I'm willing to pay you to do some work around the house, and you could ask some of the neighbors for work such as yard-mowing, baby-sitting, etc. You could have that money within a month."

The ending of the story? It could be almost anything. Perhaps Mike insisted that the guitar be a gift and refused to work. Or maybe Mike did work, but then spent his money on something else. Or perhaps Mike did work and make a down payment and then after a week or so lost interest in the guitar. Or maybe Mike became a real guitarist and started a career in music.

The important thing from our point of view is that the parents were wise enough to insist on Mike making a preliminary contribution. They were too smart to fall into the trap that catches many parents—buying expensive items that the children later do not use. Encyclopedias are perhaps the most common traps for parents. A clever salesman intrigues the children with the books, the parents pay several hundred dollars, the kids are wild about the books for three days. Some years later, they are put in a box for the Salvation Army—only about one percent of their contents having ever been used.

Bert needed money to buy a skateboard and asked his father for a loan of three dollars. He promised to pay his father back at the rate of fifty cents a week, using twenty-five cents from his fifty-cent allowance and twenty-five cents that he would earn by doing odd jobs. The arrangement worked—for two weeks. Then bickering and quarreling began. Mother got into the act, saying that Father should never have entered a financial deal with his son.

We agree! Never get into financial deals with *any* relative. It is especially bad to enter them with your children. Such deals produce nothing but trouble. Give if you will, but do not lend!

Mr. Stern caught his eleven-year-old, Buck, using the electric saber saw, which he had told Buck never to use. Father disconnected the saw and put a lock on the plug. The next time Buck went for the saber saw, he could not use it. When he asked about it, Father said, "Fine—you can use the saber saw, but you can use it only under my supervision."

When Mr. Tyler came home, he saw Joe's bicycle on its side on the grass rather than in the place where Joe had promised to keep it. They had already agreed that should Joe forget to put the bike in its proper place, he could not use it for a week. Father took the bike into the garage and tied a rope around it to remind Joe that he was not to use it for a week. Sure enough, when Joe saw the rope he knew what it meant. A week later, the father removed the rope. Thereafter Joe remembered to put the bike away when not in use.

When Mr. Dubester came home, he saw Hank's bike on its side on the grass rather than in the place where Hank had promised to keep it. They had already agreed that should Hank forget to put the bike in its proper place, Father could remind Hank to do so. Father said nothing during or after dinner. After Hank had gone to bed, Father awakened him. "What?" asked the startled Hank. "Your bike—you left it on the grass," Father said quietly, without anger. Then he left. Fifteen minutes later, he again awakened Hank and reminded him of the bike. "I don't want it anymore," Hank said. Father left but fifteen minutes later he again awakened Hank. This time Hank got angry. "I told you I don't want it anymore." "That's all right," his father said. "All I want you to do is to put it where it belongs." Hank got up grumpily, walked to the door and opened it, but then closed it and went back to bed. Fifteen minutes later, his father again awakened him. This time Hank put the bike away. The next morning, Hank used his bike as usual. He was not angry at Father.

Father awakened Hank on two other occasions that week. But after that, Hank never again forgot to put the bike away.

However—please keep this in mind—the waking technique is used *only* with the child's prior approval. Here is how Father entered the agreement with Hank:

"Hank, I am getting tired of asking you to return your bike where it belongs."

"Gee, Dad, I forget, that's all."

"You know the bike is expensive and that leaving it in the grass ruins it, and besides, the lawn looks messed up."

"Yeah, I know, Dad, but I forget."

"How would you like it if I help you to remember?"

"How?"

"If you forget, I'll remind you."

"O.K., Dad."

"Even if you are asleep, I'll remind you—not to wake you up or to punish you, but just to help you remember."

"Fine, Dad. I don't mind."

Dan had been given a rather complicated toy car with batteries and lights. His father found him working on it—that is, taking it apart. Instead of saying anything, he just looked on. When the car was disassembled, Dan began to attempt to put it together. At a glance, Father could see that this was hopeless. Dan asked Father to help. After examining the car, Father calmly told Dan that it was broken and could not be fixed. Instead of criticizing his son for breaking an expensive toy, Father had let him do as he wanted with something that was his property. And both Father and Dan profited by the experience: Father no longer bought Dan expensive toys, and Dan learned to take better care of his things.

SUMMARY

In dealing with their children about money and property, parents should follow the same principles as in dealing with anyone else. A child's money is his own.

Before parents spend a lot for an educational item for the child such as an encyclopedia or a musical instrument, they should get him to make some outlay for it, even if it is necessarily only a very modest one. Thus they are less likely to end up with something expensive that the child doesn't use.

The parent should avoid any deal with his children that involves money, especially loans. He should not become the third party in money matters involving his child.

Parents should give the child a regular allowance. The amount should be determined by the child's needs, in light of the economic condition of the family and community standards. We recommend that the parents be generous, so that the child can learn to save.

The interval between allowance payments should not be too short. With children under five, perhaps a nickel on a specified day twice a week will be fine. We recommend that when children start school, their allowances be paid once a week. The child should be given enough to pay for his school lunches during the whole week and to have left over, say, a quarter for spending money. As he gets older, dues for scouts and other inexpensive activities may be included. We recommend that at age ten, the first of the month should become the payday (however, for a while before starting monthly payments, you may want to try payday once every two weeks). The number of school days should be counted for the forthcoming month, and the amount should cover lunch, bus fare, and the like during the month, plus spending money. As the intervals between allowance payments become longer, the child has more and more reason to learn to budget his expenditures.

Each parent should have a list of "jobs" for which the child will get paid. These jobs should be work such as shining shoes, filing cards, cleaning out the car, mowing the lawn, etc.—jobs that ordinarily the parents would either do themselves or hire someone to do.

We especially recommend that the parents do not try to drive sharp bargains. Pay the child a normal rate. If, say, a garage is to be painted, get an estimate of what a regular painter would charge and then pay exactly that amount to your child if you decide to use him. Expect from him the same quality of work (or as nearly the same as he may reasonably be expected to produce). Allow him a specified time in which to finish the job. If he does poor work, quits before the job is done, or doesn't finish on time, don't pay him anything or pay him only part—do what would be fair if you were dealing with a regular painter. Incidentally, on this point and on all the others we have mentioned, it is most important that you and he reach agreement *before he starts on the job.*

In matters of money and property, common sense is what is most needed in dealing with your child. Do not make the child a beggar; do not get into deals with him; make no loans to him; let him handle his own money and property as he wishes. If the child is wasteful or destructive, do not replace items to which he did not give adequate care.

IV | INTERACTION PROBLEMS

PRELIMINARY NOTE

Problems concerning interactions in the family tend to be extremely upsetting. An angry child or parent can keep the family in a constant turmoil. Too many families live in an unhappy relationship. This is a tragedy, especially since it is relatively simple to change the relationship from tension and despair to happiness and satisfaction.

Many parents believe it is natural for children to fight and that it is necessary to attempt constant control over the children. Fortunately, there are better ways of handling fighting. A related and dangerous problem is fighting in the family automobile. And what can be more distressing to parents than children who misbehave in public? Parents have an obligation not to inflict their untrained children on others.

Training unpleasant children to become pleasant is well worth the time and effort. What greater pleasure can there be for parents than to see their children turn into friendly, cooperative, and likable people?

19 | *Fighting in the Home*

Mr. Alper had had a difficult day at the office. When he got home, he took off his shoes and stretched out on the sofa. He had just closed his eyes when the quiet was shattered by a piercing scream. With a start, Mr. Alper opened his eyes. In the dining room they were at it again: Ron and Marilyn trading blows, screeching at each other. He reclosed his eyes, hoping that the children would stop, but they didn't. In a sudden burst of anger, he scrambled to his feet and shouted, "Shut up, damn it! Both of you—*right now* —go to your rooms!" Marilyn began to complain loudly about what Ron had done to her, but Mr. Alper would have none of that. He advanced on Marilyn, his hand ready to slap. Her face contorted with anger, she retreated. Ron had disappeared into his room.

When Mr. Alper turned, his wife, who had seen what went on, said to him," "It was really Ron's fault. Marilyn was playing quietly with her doll when he came up behind her and deliberately stepped on the doll. Now Marilyn is angry with you because she thinks you were unfair." "Oh, nuts!" the father replied. "All I want is a bit of peace and quiet. Those two kids fight, fight, fight all day long. Why do they do it? Do all kids fight? I don't remember doing it with my brothers. . . ."

DISCUSSION

We have found that the commonest and most annoying problem for parents is their children's fighting. Yet fighting between children is an easy problem to handle!

Why do children fight? Both they and their parents usually believe that the fight is really over the issue that the children appear to be fighting about. Thus, in the incident just reported, Mrs. Alper thought that the reason for the fight was that Ron had stepped on Marilyn's doll. However, we believe that underneath this apparent cause there is a much more fundamental one—what one might call the *real* reason. *Children usually fight to keep their parents busy and involved with them.* They themselves are rarely aware of this, nevertheless we believe it to be the case: *their basic purpose in fighting is usually to get their parents' attention.*

To end fighting, parents must simply keep the children from achieving this fundamental purpose.

Incidentally, we must make clear that we do not disapprove of fighting per se. Children, in our view, have a right to fight. However, they have no right, in fighting, to disturb others who are not disturbing them. Certainly Marilyn had a right to fight with Ron because he deliberately stepped on her doll. But she had no right to bother her father.

SOLUTION

We offer three ways to deal with children's fights. We suggest that you routinely use the first method to the limit that, for you, is supportable or seems advisable. When that method is inapplicable or proves ineffective, use the second or, if that seems unsuitable or proves ineffective, the third.

Bear it—Remember: they are only kids; they are trying to learn how to deal with life; their bickerings and quarrelings are their way of learning to solve their problems. Just be quiet, let the kids have their fight, and say nothing. Sooner or later, they will stop.

Beat it—Don't be an audience. Go into the bathroom or some other room. When the quarrel is over, you simply come back in silence.

"Boot" them out—Put all offenders out the door into the yard or street. However, you must do this precisely in this manner:
1. Say to them: "If you are going to fight, you must go outside. When you are through, come back in." Don't say it again.
2. If they do not go outside, put them out in *complete silence!*
3. From then on if you use the third method, do it in *complete silence!*

SOLUTION APPLIED TO THE ALPERS

When the Alpers were told of these methods, both were skeptical. Father shook his head. "You don't know how hostile these kids are," he said. However, both agreed to try our suggestions. Their first step was to talk to the kids. Marilyn and Ron listened carefully. Within fifteen minutes there was an uproar. Both parents looked on and said nothing. The bickering continued for several minutes and then Marilyn ran over to her mother. "Ron has my shoe box and he won't give it to me."

Mother was about to ask Ron to give Marilyn back her shoe box but reflected: I'll get into a fight with him too if I ask him. So she said nothing and just looked at her angry daughter. "Did you hear me, Mother? Make him give me back *my* shoe box!" Marilyn demanded.

Mrs. Alper didn't know what to do. It was uncomfortable just looking and saying nothing. Then she had an inspiration.

"I couldn't find one of my earrings this morning," she said.

Her seven-year-old daughter looked at her contemptuously.

"I said Ron has my shoe box."

"And I said I couldn't find my earring," Mother said clearly. Both father and brother were listening to this weird conversation.

"And I don't care about your old earring," Marilyn said. "I want back my shoe box."

"I'm sorry you don't care about my earring; it means a lot to me," Mother persisted.

Her daughter turned her back to Mother and went to her room. There was peace for an hour, an almost unprecedented event in this family. Then both children got into another hassle. Almost as one, the two parents rose and walked out of the house into the front yard. As soon as the door was closed, the battle ended. The parents talked a bit, and Father commented that it was certainly interesting that the fight, whatever it was about, had ended when they, the parents, left.

Mr. and Mrs. Williams complained that they had to have a baby-sitter when they left the house because their fourteen-year-old son was brutal to his ten-year-old sister; the parents were afraid to leave the two alone. The parents were advised to use our methods and to leave the kids alone without a baby-sitter.

When the parents discussed this with their children, Mollie said, "He'll kill me!"

Mother replied, "I'm sure he will not hurt you if you don't bother him."

That very night, for the first time, the parents left the children alone. When they came back, both kids were watching television.

A mother complained that her four-year-old son, Jimmy, so "hated" his baby brother, Billy, that he was always deliberately hurting him. "I'm afraid he's a sadist," Mother said. She was advised to "ignore it," but she stated she couldn't stand her four-year-old's "torturing" the four-month-old. She was advised nevertheless to "beat it" (i.e., leave them alone) and see what happened. It was also recommended to her that she have a playtime with Jimmy and give him then much positive attention and encouragement.

She reported the next day that when Jimmy pinched the sleeping Billy, the baby awoke and screamed so loudly that Jimmy got frightened and ran to Mother. Mother said nothing to Jimmy. Jimmy asked why Billy cried. Although Mother knew Jimmy had pinched his brother, she answered, "Maybe he's hungry. Should we feed him?"

A week later, she reported that Jimmy no longer was pinching Billy. Then she told the following horror story:

"For several days, Jimmy kept annoying Billy. Each time Billy would cry and Jimmy would get scared, so I realized that the baby could take care of himself. And so I didn't interfere, realizing that if I did, I'd be giving Jimmy attention for his misbehavior and encouraging him to be worse. After four days he stopped annoying Billy. But the next day I saw him with a knife. It's only a toy plastic knife, but it could hurt. Jimmy had it in his hand, and he walked stealthily over to where Billy was sleeping in his crib. He put the hand with the knife inside the crib bars, and then he raised his hand as though to bring the knife down on his sleeping brother. I don't know what kept me from dashing over and grabbing Jimmy, but I just looked on. And Jimmy brought the toy knife down on Billy—but he did it so slowly and touched Billy so lightly that Billy didn't even wake up.

"I heaved a sigh of relief and realized that *he had been doing all this just for my benefit.* From now on I am not going to worry about Jimmy hurting Billy."

SUMMARY

We don't like fights; but if children want to fight, we let them do it, *provided* they do it in a place where it doesn't bother other people. Our experience has been that fighting almost always stops or diminishes rapidly if our methods are used. We have had no serious difficulties with children hurting one another. As a matter of fact, the methods of intervention used by most parents are much more likely to lead to bloody noses and scratched faces than are our methods.

If you have fighting children, use our methods consistently: Bear it, beat it, or "boot" them out. If you give them attention because of their fighting, you are giving them what they are fighting for. Stop lecturing, punishing, sending children to their room, or otherwise "rewarding" children for fighting!

20 | *Fighting in the Car*

On their vacation, Mr. and Mrs. Rawl were speeding along a freeway at the legal limit. Suddenly Jon and Roberta, in the back seat, began to quarrel, hitting at each other. Mr. Rawl's temper was short due to the heat and the tension of driving. "Stop it!" he shouted. The fighting abated for a moment, and then it erupted again. Mr. Rawl turned around, holding the wheel with his left hand, his right hand seeking someone to slap. As he hit one of the children, his left hand pulled the wheel and the car swerved. Mrs. Rawl screamed and grabbed the wheel. The car nearly went out of control; it was indeed fortunate that a serious accident did not occur. The entire family, shaken by the experience, quieted down for a while. The parents wondered if they should ever drive again with the kids.

DISCUSSION

Some fifty thousand people are killed annually in the United States in automobile accidents. The number caused by fighting children is, of course, unknown. But we can be sure that there are auto deaths due to this problem.

Parents' reaction usually is to yell at the children. This generally works for only a little while. Some parents stop the car and spank the children. This frequently makes them even wilder and leads to a still bigger blowup the next time. Making them promise to behave, having some up front and some in the back—these are makeshift measures that do not really solve the problem.

SOLUTION

1. Talk with the children at a time when everyone is calm, perhaps just before the auto trip. Explain what you intend to do should they make a fuss and start quarreling in the car: you will stop the car until they calm down. Having explained this so that they understand, do not repeat it later. From now on you are going to act and not talk.
2. Should a disturbance occur while driving, pull to the side of the road as soon as convenient, and wait in silence until they calm down. If they start bothering you with comments or complaints while you are waiting, get out of the car, and return only when they have subsided. When all is calm—this may take as little as two minutes or as long as several hours—without saying anything, start again.
3. Once you have started, should they again begin to fight, stop—and this time allow calmness to prevail awhile before driving off again. They may miss doctors' appointments or be late to school; the more inconvenient the wait for all concerned, the more it will impress on the children that their car behavior must be changed. You may, if it seems advisable, return home at this point.
4. Do not discuss the incident at all while driving or afterwards.
5. Should still another outburst of fighting occur, stop as soon as possible and wait as long as necessary for the calming down.

SOLUTION APPLIED TO THE RAWL FAMILY

After learning our solution for fighting in the car, Mr. and Mrs. Rawl talked to their children, explaining what would happen should they fight in the car on their next excursion. The children did not pay much attention to their parents' words and, during the next car ride, they started fighting. Mr. Rawl silently pulled over to the side of the road and waited. The startled children asked, "Why are we sitting here?" Father did not answer. When they were quiet and he felt calm, he started driving again. The children were quiet for a while but soon started up again. Father turned back toward home, ending the planned family outing.

The following weekend, parents and children decided it would be nice to visit the grandparents, who lived about twenty-five miles away. The family got into the car without anything being said about fighting. The children kept themselves amused, Jon counting all the green cars and Roberta counting all the red cars. It was a very pleasant drive.

FURTHER EXAMPLES

Mr. Thomas and his fiancée, Mrs. Russell, were driving. In the back seat were Mrs. Russell's children, Will and Anne, two battlers. (Mrs. Russell, a divorcee, was at the moment a very fearful woman. One of her former husband's tendencies had been to get very excited if the kids began fighting. He would harangue them while driving, thereby upsetting her.) Suddenly the children began to hit each other and scream. Mr. Thomas pulled to the side of the road. With the fighting still going on, he opened his door and got out of the car, motioning to his fiancée to come too. They walked down the block and entered a store. About five minutes later, Anne showed up, and five minutes after that, Will did too. Nothing was said. All four got into the car and continued. After several such incidents, fighting in the car finally stopped.

On vacation, Mr. and Mrs. Mayher and their children, in bathing suits, were en route to a beach. The children were tremendous battlers and, sure enough, they began whaling away at each other. Father pulled the car to the curb. The fighting stopped immediately. "Why did you stop?" Joseph asked, since this was a new procedure. "I will not drive when I am upset," Father said, "and only when I am calmed down will I continue." They waited a few minutes and then one of the kids said irritably, "Let's go." Father got out of the car and walked away. Mother joined him.

"This nonsense has got to stop," Father said. "I think we ought to give them a good lesson." Mother agreed, and the two of them walked about for a while. About fifteen minutes later, they returned to the car. The children were silent. Father started the car. Within a block, fighting resumed. Father pulled to the curb and took out the keys. He and his wife left the car. The two children looked defiantly at their parents. The time was 10 A.M. At 3 P.M., the parents returned. They found one child stretched out on the grassy patch near the sidewalk, the other stretched out on the car seat. The parents got in and drove to the beach.

That was the very last car fight they ever had.

"I want to warn all you kids that from now on, if there's any fighting in the car—I don't care who starts it—we pull over to the side of the road to calm down, and we may go back home," Mother stated to their five kids, age five to eleven. Father nodded. Each child stated that he understood. Fighting in the car stopped almost completely. Father had to pull over to the side of the road for a few minutes only once or twice.

One Saturday the family piled into their station wagon to go to the circus. About a quarter of the way there, a fight started between the eight-year-old and the nine-year-old. Father made a right turn and headed back home. "Why?" wailed the eleven-year-old. "We didn't start it. They did. Why should all of us have to go back home?"

The parents did not answer. They parked the car and went into the house. All five children were crying bitterly, the eight-year-old and the nine-year-old each blaming the other, and the rest complaining that they were innocent and didn't deserve this treatment. The parents did not reply. They were training their children about what could be a matter of life or death. After this experience, the five chldren did not fight in the car, and the family had many fine outings.

SUMMARY

The method of logical consequences when applied as we have recommended has, in our experience, been invariably successful in ending fighting in the car.

21 | *Behavior in Public*

Mr. Copi invited the Kents for a Sunday cruise and added, "Bring your kids along. I'm sure they'll enjoy it." He was wrong. No one enjoyed the sail—not even the four Kent children. This is what occurred:

Steve and Wendy got into a loud screaming battle.

Susan cried because there was no milk on the boat.

Greg got the boat lines all tangled up.

Mother annoyed the Copis with her yelling "Don't" and "Stop that."

Steve was found rummaging around below decks, opening drawers.

Greg dropped a winch handle overboard after his mother had said, "Don't touch it." Mr. Copi said, "That's nothing," but he well knew it was a forty-dollar loss.

A miserable time was had by everyone. Mr. Copi swore silently that he would never invite those kids again—ever. His wife was driven practically to tears by these bad-tempered children and their shrewish mother. Mr. Kent became almost murderously angry, and when they got home he gave each kid a licking. This disastrous experience was long remembered.

A year later, the family was invited to spend a week with relatives. "How can we accept this invitation?" Mrs. Kent asked her husband. "Our kids are completely undisciplined. Wherever we take them, they act up—getting into things, fighting, demanding, crying. I just don't see how we can accept the invitation."

"Damn it," Mr. Kent muttered. "Some families have outings and visits, and the kids behave beautifully. Why on earth don't we have such kids? What can we do to make them behave? Nothing seems to work, not even hard spankings."

His wife replied, "I just don't know why they act that way. They aren't so bad at home, but when we take them out they're impossible. I wonder if it's because when we're out they know you won't hit them, and they take advantage of this."

"Whatever the reason, we have to do something about it," Father stated. "I am ready to do anything—just anything—to get these kids under control. Why don't you check with some other families or call some doctor or someone to see what can be done."

DISCUSSION

It sometimes happens that children are "good" in the home and "bad" outside. Frequently, school personnel are told, "I can't understand why my Bobby isn't getting along at school. We have no trouble at all with him at home."

Such children are often cowed by their parents, who rule by force and terror. Children constantly controlled by their parents usually have no self-control. They "go wild" and misbehave if the school gives greater freedom.

SOLUTION

1. The children should be told (when they are quiet and listening) the kind of behavior expected of them and the *logical consequences should they misbehave.*
2. Families should playact training situations for specific problems such as eating properly in a restaurant.
3. Parents should first "experiment" with the outside behavior in situations where failure may not be disastrous. Friends or relatives may be called upon to help.

4. The consequences, if there are violations, must be applied immediately, decisively, and in silence.

SOLUTION APPLIED TO THE KENT FAMILY

Mrs. Kent went to an Adlerian family counselor, who suggested a plan for dealing with the problem. She later discussed this plan, and they agreed to put it into action.

They called the children and said, "We want to tell you in advance how we expect you to behave if ever we go out. And we want you to understand that if you don't behave properly, we'll go right home." Then they explained specifically what they did not want: whining, fighting, crying, making demands, looking in closets or drawers, touching things that are prohibited, and so on.

Wendy asked what would happen if only one of them misbehaved. Mother said, "If anyone misbehaves, we'll all come home." Wendy replied, "That isn't fair. If I'm playing nicely, why should I have to go home?" Father added, "If it's convenient, I may stay or Mother may stay, and some of you may stay too. But if it's so far away that we have gone in the car, then the whole family will have to return."

Having made sure that everyone understood, Mr. and Mrs. Kent put their training procedure into practice. They suggested having a picnic at a beach. They were going to have a fire, cook frankfurters, and roast marshmallows. Mrs. Kent bought a small air cushion raft.

Before leaving, the parents gave the children specific instructions:
—No fighting
—No crying
—Always stay in sight
—No whining

The children said that they understood. Father then said, "If anyone misbehaves, we all come home. Do you understand?"

And they took off. It was a two-hour ride to the beach, and they got there about eleven. A fire was started, food was taken out, the kids ran into the water. About twelve-thirty, Mother called that the meal was ready; the kids, famished, came to eat. Suddenly there was an explosion: a fight between Wendy and Susan over who was to have the first frankfurter. Other people nearby looked on in surprise at the intensity of the fight. Mr. Kent looked at his wife and nodded. She quickly began to pack. Father deflated the raft and started to carry things back to the car. He threw the frankfurters into a garbage can. Within minutes they were ready to leave. The astonished children, shocked to find the parents' warning coming true, got into the car; the family returned without a stop, getting home in the early afternoon, with everyone hungry, thirsty, tired, and subdued.

The parents felt that the lesson had been learned. They repeated the same expedition the following week, going through the same routine. That day was just perfect.

However, the Kents knew that there was more to be done. One day, Mrs. Reinhardt called. Her family was having a birthday party, to which she invited the Kent children. The conversation went as follows:

"Marge, you know what a nuisance my kids are."

"Oh, Myra, they're normal."

"I hope so. But they are quite a nuisance outside the home. Anyhow, here is what I want to ask you. I am now training them. I want to ask you to promise that if we come to the birthday party and any one of my kids misbehaves, you won't interfere if I take him home immediately."

"All right, if that's what you want. Actually, I think it's a good idea. Your kids do sometimes get a little rough."

The next Saturday, as the children were in the car about to go to the party, Father turned around to talk to them.

"If any one of you doesn't want to go, let me know and I'll stay home with you, and Mother will drive the others."

The kids all demanded to go, wondering why their father was even asking them.

"If anyone misbehaves at the party, I'll take him or her home immediately. Understand?"

Each of the kids indicated understanding.

Mother added. "If Father has to take anyone home, and then someone else misbehaves, I'll take *everyone* home." Again the kids nodded understanding.

They drove off and, sure enough, not long after they arrived,

Greg got into a battle with Barry Reinhardt about a toy. Mr. Kent scooped up Greg, and within a minute both were in the car going home, with Greg carrying on in a violent temper tantrum. The rest of the kids had a wonderful time—something that they reported enthusiastically on their return.

When summer arrived, the Kent family spent a weekend with their distant relatives, who complimented the parents on "their wonderful children." The Kents looked at each other and smiled, feeling that their training efforts had really paid off.

FURTHER EXAMPLES

The Hams went out for dinner with their eleven-year-old son and twelve-year-old daughter. At the restaurant, both children started jostling each other to sit at Mother's right side. The parents, who had been counseled regarding such behavior, got up and went to another table. The kids looked on in confusion. When the waiter came, Father said, "Is it possible for us to sit at one table and our kids at another?" The waiter, who had seen the situation, said, "Of course." The two pairs, separated, ate in peace.

That was the last time the kids ever pulled that kind of behavior in public.

The Malterre family went to a summer resort with their two children, five and six. Mrs. Malterre noted that the kids were splashing people in the pool, much to their annoyance. She got up, called to the children, and started to walk away from the pool. The children, afraid to be left alone, followed her, asking why they were leaving. Mother said nothing until she was some distance from the pool.

"I didn't want to talk to you while at the pool," she said. "You are disturbing others, splashing water. Either you stop this, or we'll go back to our cabin."

Both kids promised to stop. They returned to the pool, where no further trouble arose.

That evening at the dinner table, the children started "fooling around"—getting up and down, making noises, and in other ways annoying the other guests. Mother got up, called the kids, and walked back to the cabin with them. She waited for Father, who arrived after having eaten. Mother then returned to the table for her meal. She finished her dinner in peace, and returned to the cabin.

Meanwhile the children were quiet, realizing how they had inconvenienced their parents. They behaved properly at table for the rest of the vacation.

Whenever the Guralnicks went out to eat, they were embarrassed by the behavior of their two children. The kids simply had unrefined eating habits. The parents had a discussion and evolved a plan.

"We'd like to go out to Sanderson's Steak House," Father said to the family, "but I will not go unless you kids know how to eat properly."

There was a lot of discussion about whether or not the children ate properly. The kids wanted to go there particularly because you could select your steak and cook it yourself.

Finally Father said, "Well, I'll take you, but only on the condition that you show me whether or not you can eat properly. And this means really properly. I'll make out I am the waiter, and I want you two kids to show me how you eat. Mother can watch and make notes, and later she will tell you what she thinks you did wrong, if you did anything wrong. If you both eat properly, then we'll go to Sanderson's."

The kids agreed, and at their next meal Father acted the role of waiter. The table was set as at a restaurant. The kids had to get their own salad at a salad bar. When the kids finished their meal, Mother gave her impressions.

"David, when you got to the table, you didn't help your sister, and you sat down first. You didn't put your napkin on your lap. And you were kicking her under the table. Alice, you were playing with your water glass, and you spilled some salad off your plate and spilled some milk on the table. But otherwise you did fine."

Father added, "Well, you did pretty well. Next meal, we'll have another trial, and when you both show you can eat properly, we'll all go to eat at Sanderson's."

SUMMARY

Parents have an obligation to prepare their children for social behavior, and usually the most important factor in such preparation is that the parents themselves act properly.

Children should be shown the way in which to act; they should be informed of the consequences of misbehavior. Consequences should be applied immediately, in silence and in a firm manner, without anger, threats, or scoldings. If others in the family have to be discomfited, this is the price of training. It is a small price to pay for having pleasant family outings and visits.

22 | *Aggression*

When Mr. Niedzielski came home, his three-year-old son ran to him to be picked up and hugged. "Did you bring me something?" little Beau asked.

"No, son, nothing today."

"Bad Daddy!" Beau shouted, and hit his father.

"I don't know where he got this," Mother stated, "but he is becoming very aggressive. He hits other children, and now he hits me when I tell him to do something."

"Oh, Doris, it's probably just a stage. Maybe he wants attention. Why don't you give him more love?"

"I don't know about that. He gets a lot of love. If he doesn't get his way, he is so angry that he hits. I think he'd better learn to control his temper or he will have trouble in life."

DISCUSSION

Aggression, whether physical or verbal, is common in children. The aggression may be selective—only to the family, or to other relatives, or to animals, or to younger children; or it can be quite general—toward anyone or anything that frustrates or angers the child.

151

The four goals of children's misbehavior (see Chapter 2) can give us insight into the nonconscious purposes a child may have for aggressive behavior: (1) I want attention and one way to get it is to hit others; (2) I want to be powerful—everyone must do just what I want, otherwise I will hit them; (3) I hate everyone and want to get even—I'll hit everybody I can; or (4) I just can't control myself—when I'm angry I just have to hit. I can't help myself.

Aggression, then, may be not only a response to a frustration or a disappointment but a sign of the child's general attitude.

SOLUTION

1. Talk to the child at a time when he is calm. Tell him that you do not like his behavior and would be happy if he would stop it.

Do not ask the child why he hits others, because children almost never know the actual why. Express your feelings and tell him what you intend to do if he continues such behavior.

2. After due warning, if he shows aggressive behavior, react by appropriate counter-behavior *immediately*. If he hits you, you should hit him back right then and there—if possible, at the very moment he hits you. So if you see him cocking his fist, have your hand ready: as his fist hits you, your hand hits him. If he hits you on the leg, strike back at him, preferably at his leg (you may have to hit him on the hand, shoulder, or arm to be instantaneous). Regulate the force of your slap according to the amount of force he uses. The slap or returned kick should be painful enough to make him aware of the reaction he has engendered but not more painful or hurtful than that. Remember you are using a training technique. Your reaction should not proceed from anger; if you can smile, he will see that you are not angry. You simply want to *teach* him that hitting hurts.

A slap on the bottom is *not* suggested. That would be punishment; it would tell the child that you cold-bloodedly hit him on his rear because of what he did—he would feel that you do not like him. It is important for him to know that you like him but do not like what he does; this should not be said in words—only shown in action.

This advice may *seem* to contradict our general nonpunitive attitude. However, the action we recommend is not punitive. It is an example of logical consequences. The parent shows respect for self and respect for the child. The principle is: If you hit me, then I'll hit you. You hit in silence, and he experiences that hitting is unpleasant, even painful.

It would be punishment if, after the child hit the parent, the parent said or did one of the following:

—"You are going to go to hell for such behavior. Don't you know what the commandment says about honoring your father and your mother?..."

—"For the next week you can't watch TV."

—"All right. You hit me. That does it. I won't bring home candy from now on."

—"Do that once more and I'll hit you so hard you'll never hit me again."

—Get a paddle or strap and then beat him.

These reactions would be punishment. They involve anger, dislike, violence. The child would feel that he is bad. If showing a smile is not possible, at least be poker-faced and show no animosity by your expression. But if you are hurt (and even a young child can hurt terribly), you may show, on being struck, your immediate reaction of dismay, surprise, or pain. However, when hitting him, show no anger—smile or be poker-faced.

Note: It is important for the parents, when using such training techniques, to give positive, loving attention in daily play when the child behaves well. Parents should never withhold love while training.

SOLUTION APPLIED TO BEAU

After dinner, the parents talked to their son as follows:

"Beau, from now on, if you hit us we will hit you back. It is not good to hit people. If you hit children, they will not like you. They will run away from you, and won't play with you. So don't hit anymore. But if you do hit us, we will hit you."

Later that night, when Mother told Beau it was bedtime, he ran to hit her. To his surprise, as his fist struck her, her palm got him right on the face with a stinging blow. Enraged, he raised his fist and struck again, and Mother struck back, a bit harder this time. He showed surprise and again raised his hand. Mother had her hand up, awaiting Beau, ready to hit if he hit. He stopped! The two looked at each other.

"I'm sorry, Mommy," Beau suddenly said.

"I'm sorry too," Mrs. Niedzielski replied, and took him in her arms. "Come, let us go to bed now." She read him a story as usual and kissed him good night.

The next evening, Father again did not bring anything home for Beau, and Beau again raised his fist. Father opened his hand, ready to slap if Beau hit. Beau looked up: "You going to hit a little kid?" Father, who thought this statement very funny, replied, "If you hit a big man, the big man is going to hit the little kid." Then Beau said, "This little kid isn't going to hit the big man." Father said, "Good," and picked him up and gave him a hug.

Within three days Beau ceased to display aggression against his parents. The immediate appropriate physical reactions on their part told the child clearly that if he inflicted pain on others, they would respond in a way unpleasant for him.

FURTHER EXAMPLES

Four-year-old Izzy suddenly started spitting at people. The parents went through the routine we recommended to them. They explained to him their feelings about spitting and told him what they would do if he continued to spit at others: they would give him an immediate slap.

To spit back would not have been appropriate: it is demeaning and disrespectful to spit at anyone; besides, spitting back may seem to the child a game and may induce him to continue. To slap within a twentieth of a second after the spitting is a far better procedure.

Izzy gave up spitting at people within a day.

Three-year-old Teddy started biting people. As Mother held him one day, he bit her on the arm. She very quickly bit *his* arm. He was startled, but bit her again. She bit him again, this time a little harder. He started to cry. Mother, with a pleasant expression on her face, put him down. When he stopped crying, she sat on the floor and played with him; later she held him on her lap and cuddled him.

Mother showed respect for herself by not allowing Teddy to hurt her, and respect for the child by not yelling, punishing, or permitting him to get by with inappropriate behavior. She did not withhold love or make him feel that he was a bad kid. She simply allowed him to experience the consequences of biting others. She acted quickly and in silence. She then played with him when he was behaving well and demonstrated her love. Teddy stopped biting people; Mother and Teddy maintained their good relationship.

Mrs. Bonner heard screaming and looked out the window. Michael, Mrs. Bonner's five-year-old son, had just hit Janine, a neighbor's daughter, who was three. This was the second time that day he had done so. She had talked to Michael, but it obviously hadn't helped. She went over to see Janine's mother and said, "If you ever see Michael bothering or hitting your Janine, please take care of it. You have my authority to talk to him, to warn him not to do it anymore. Tell him that you won't let Janine play with him, and call me so I can take him in. If I'm not around, please take Janine away from Michael."

With a concerted effort between the two mothers, Michael's aggressive behavior ended in a short time.

When Mrs. Martin saw Tim, age four, twisting his knuckles on baby sister Phyllis's head and making her cry, her first impulse was to protect Phyllis, but she wisely did nothing. Phyllis's crying scared Tim and he stopped.

SUMMARY

Our usual training methods—ignoring inappropriate behavior or using natural and logical consequences—do not always work with a child who becomes aggressive. Hence we suggest a firm counterattack technique.

23 | *Undesirable Companions*

THE PROBLEM

"Come right in, Helene!" Mrs. Jacobs called out.

Obediently, her daughter left her friend and came in.

"Why, Mama?" she asked.

"I don't want you to play with Renee."

"But why, Mama? We have such fun."

"Mother knows best, Helene. You are only ten. I want you to play with nice kids. Why don't you play with the Schwartz children?"

"They're too young."

"Well, then, play with the La Brie children."

"I don't like them."

Mother became exasperated. "Well, I don't want to see you with Renee. And if I do see you talking or playing with her again, I'm going to bring you into the house and you'll have to stay in your room the rest of the day."

"But, Ma, it just isn't fair." And Helene began to cry.

DISCUSSION

Children grow up in three arenas—the home, the school, and the street. Parents must train the child in the home and then allow the child to manage school and street problems by himself.

The choice of friends tells a great deal about a child. If he plays only with younger children, we may conclude that he feels inferior to kids his size and age. He may want to boss younger children. Perhaps he is a born "mother" and wants to instruct and protect little children. That he plays with older children may indicate that he is looking upward, is ambitious, and wants to be big. Or he may be merely playing the kid-brother role.

On the street the child really begins to be on his own. There he can begin to express himself as an individual with more latitude than he has either at home or at school. No longer is he under the direct control of adults—he can become himself. With his peers he begins to develop his social being.

On the street the child at first cautiously explores the big wonderful terrifying world of the "outside." He may be hurt by others. He encounters new attitudes. Should he say, "My mother says . . ." he finds himself derided. He is placed in his first loyalty conflict. If he is on the side of his home and family, he is laughed at. At times he must become a traitor, not mentioning mother . . . and later teacher, denying their wisdom and advice and admonitions. He soon becomes two personalities: he has his street self and his home self, each with its own vocabularly.

How surprised parents are when they learn from others the image their child has in the street.

"What!" shrieks the mother when she learns that her son is the neighborhood bully, carries a portfolio of *Playboy* pictures, is the chief tormentor of new kids, is giving free consultations in applied gynecology, instructs in commando techniques, and is the one who deflated Mr. Warfel's car tires last week. Mother is almost in shock as she listens to this "authentic" description, trying to reconcile the boy she knows with this neighborhood monster.

Some children will not go out to play in the street because of their inability to adjust to the world outside. They will obediently sit in front of the house and deal only with "nice" children. Subdued by their parents, they do not learn to deal with life, and they tend to become fearful and discouraged.

Our golden rule regarding the child when he starts to go out:

"Leave him alone." Let him find his own friends and explore relationships. Young Ronald will be with Franklin this week, with Walter the next, with James the next, and then back to Franklin. These pairings are a kind of mating and, like all voluntary matings, are based on a complex of compatibility factors.

No parent is wise enough to know which of the kids his child goes with are "good" or which are "bad." Isolating a child is not the answer. If the parent has taught his child basic values, the child should be able to meet life without being corrupted, and the parent need not worry.

There is at least one child in every neighborhood who is a "bad" child: sexually precocious, a thief, a liar, a troublemaker. Every parent in the neighborhood would be happy to make a contribution to a moving-away present should this monster leave the area.

SOLUTION

What should be done about such a child?

Adopt him! Invite him into your home—feed him, play with him, treat him with love, kindness, and respect—so that he, like your own child, gets the benefit of your warmth and good sense. Do not be dismayed if he does not know how to behave. Do not be upset if he "attacks" you—wild animals will do that before they are tamed. Be ready to see him melt and become normal, sweet, and good. Thus you will be helping your own child and another parent's child as well.

SOLUTION APPLIED TO HELENE

Mrs. Jacobs noticed that Helene was now playing out of sight and becoming more secretive. She realized that her daughter was probably still playing with that naughty Renee. So Mother went to a trusted friend for advice. After initial resistance to the advice, Mother realized that it did make sense, and the following occurred that night:

"Helene, I'd like you to invite some of your friends over for ice cream and cookies."

"Why, Mama?"

"I think it would be a nice thing to do. You can ask some kids from the neighborhood and from school. And please be sure to invite Renee."

"Renee? I thought you didn't . . . I mean, I don't . . . Why do you want her?"

"I changed my mind about her. I'd like to meet her and be friendly with her. Do you think she would come?"

"I don't know."

"Helene, please ask her to come over and talk with me later today. I'd like to invite her myself."

A half hour later, Helene and Renee appeared together, and Mrs. Jacobs graciously invited Renee to the little party. Both kids withdrew, puzzled.

"I thought you said your mother didn't want you to play with me," Renee said to Helene.

"I thought she didn't. I don't understand her."

"Yeah, parents are funny. Let's play house. . . ."

As a result of Mrs. Jacobs's change of attitude, Renee became a frequent visitor to the Jacobs home. She began to feel at home there, and the two girls played nicely. Other children, some of whom had been told by their parents to avoid Renee, also began to play with her. One day a neighbor came by and talked with Mrs. Jacobs.

"I notice that Helene is playing with Renee," said Mrs. Van Natta.

"Oh, yes. I used to forbid her to play with Renee, but I found out that she was not doing as I wished. So I decided to give her permission to do what she was doing anyway. Renee is a human being and it's wrong for us adults to ostracize her. I can see that she is changing. I think we all should feel responsible and should welcome her. Don't you agree?"

"Maybe you're right. We've been making her an outcast. I'll tell my Lori she can play with Renee. Thank you for making me see it differently."

SUMMARY

Parents should allow their children freedom in the arena of the street. In every community there is likely to be at least one "bad" child. It is natural for parents to want to shield their children from the unwholesome influence of such a child, but to try to do so is a mistake. We hope that parents will instead try to help the "bad" child to become "good" by opening their home to him and encouraging him to become more cooperative. You may not know it, but another parent may think that *your* children are "bad."

24 | *Demanding Too Much Attention*

The phone rang. Mrs. Knox, who had been cooking, dried her hands to answer. It was her friend Arlene. As the two ladies were starting a pleasant conversation, four-year-old Pam came running in from the yard and began pulling on Mother's skirt, shouting something about a doll. "Just a minute, Arlene," Mrs. Knox said. She turned to her daughter. "You shouldn't bother me when I'm on the phone." The girl screamed louder about not finding her doll. The exasperated mother went back to the phone. "We have a crisis," she said. "I'll call you later." She hung up the phone and looked at her daughter. "That's about the tenth time this week you have interfered with me when I was on the telephone. When will you learn to wait? Now, what is it that you want?" And after hearing Pam's complaint, Mrs. Knox went looking for the doll. Later she called her friend back and apologized saying, "I just don't know how to get her to stop interfering with me when I'm on the phone."

DISCUSSION

Some children's main goal in life is getting attention. Parents should train children to know that there is a time to get attention and a time not to and that they should get attention by useful rather than by useless means. The trick is to learn how to give children the attention they desire but not to succumb to misbehavior such as force or blackmail.

SOLUTION

1. Decide whether or not the child's behavior is an attempt to get undue attention.
2. Think of a proper logical consequence. Ignoring or withdrawing from the behavior will usually work.
3. Inform the child that his behavior bothers you and that you intend not to pay attention when you are bothered. Tell him that you will listen to him and play with him when he is pleasant. Say these things only once.
4. Put your idea into practice. Be calm and quiet, firm and friendly.
5. Continue your procedure consistently, as long as necessary.

SOLUTION APPLIED TO THE KNOX FAMILY

Mrs. Knox said calmly, "Pam, from now on, when I am on the telephone I don't want you to bother me. I will just not pay attention to you."

Surprised at her mother's calmness, Pam answered, "Yes, Mommy."

Mrs. Knox next called the friend with whom she had most of her conversations. "Listen, Arlene: if I ever mention 'camels' in our phone conversation, you'll know I am dealing with Pam, so you can hang up even though I remain at the phone. I'll pretend that I'm talking to you, while I ignore her."

Several days later, while Mother was on the telephone, Pam ran over and began pulling on her mother's dress. Mrs. Knox hurriedly mentioned "camels" and her friend said, "I'll listen in—don't be concerned about me." A rather unusual scene was then enacted, with Mrs. Knox talking more or less nonsense into the receiver and trying to control herself while Pam shouted and yelled and tugged.

Mrs. Knox determinedly talked on. Suddenly Pam changed tactics and began pounding Mother with her fist. Mrs. Knox hung up the receiver and walked to the bathroom and locked herself in. Pam began pounding on the door, shouting. Mrs. Knox turned on the radio. The baffled and indignant Pam began hammering on the door, screaming wildly. Mrs. Knox started a long bath. The pounding ended. Mrs. Knox finished her bath and went back into the living room. Pam was reading a book and looked up. "Hi, sweetheart," Mother said sweetly. She picked up the telephone again, dialed her friend, and reopened their conversation, saying nothing about the incident with Pam.

In the next two weeks, Pam and Mother repeated this performance several times. Then Pam's excessive demands for attention ended.

FURTHER EXAMPLES

Mrs. Calia reported that her six-year-old, Vincent, was a daredevil and would do dangerous things when she took him to a playground. He liked to make the swing go high or to climb to the top of the jungle-gym and stand up; he also did other hazardous things.

The counselor asked her what *she* did. She replied that she told her son to come down, or to stop it, or to come to her—and that she once even climbed up to get him.

The counselor gave her a simple suggestion: "Turn your back." Vincent soon realized that Mother wasn't looking—and what was the use of acting if she paid no attention? So he gave up the nonsense and stopped his dangerous activities.

Mrs. Calia had not realized that by giving him attention she was provoking her child to do dangerous things.

Often when two-year-old Betty was placed in her bed at naptime, she would get out of bed and make a mess in the room—out of the cabinets would come all the toys, books, and clothes. Mother would scold Betty. And Mother began to think that the child didn't need a nap even though she seemed tired.

Mother enrolled in one of our Family Education Centers. The

counselor told her that Betty still needed naps but that she had found a way to get much attention from Mother. Mother was told to put Betty in bed, to do nothing to keep her in bed, and to keep the door to her room closed. If Betty got out of the room, she was to be brought back in silence. A timer or alarm clock set for one hour was to be in the room; when it rang, Betty could come out. If there was a mess, Mother was not to say a word about it; she was not to ask Betty to clean it up, she was not to scold or spank. At a later time, when Betty was occupied, Mother would put things away.

Within two weeks Betty was napping quietly.

The Kefir family was in a rush in the mornings since both parents worked and the children had to be driven to the day care center. Three-year-old Sandy got a lot of attention every morning in that she was constantly being told to hurry. She was slow in dressing and seldom had time to eat breakfast. At the last minute, either Mother or Father ended up dressing her after much nagging, scolding, or spanking.

The parents were advised by the family counselor to tell Sandy only once that it was her job to get ready in the mornings, that they were not going to dress her, and that if necessary, they would put her, undressed, into the car with her clothes, and she could either dress herself or go into her class undressed. On the days when Mother drove, Sandy found that she really was adamant about not dressing her daughter—Sandy learned to dress herself on those days. But Father felt sorry for Sandy and on the days when he drove he would dress her at the last minute; Sandy learned to anticipate this. When Father stopped feeling sorry for his little girl and giving her this service, she quickly began dressing herself.

SUMMARY

There is only one answer: ignore the child when he demands undue attention. Continue with whatever you are doing. Do not talk, scold, or respond in any way to this misbehavior. If you become upset because the child gets your goat, walk away—go into the bathroom, turn the radio on, do not listen to the child, come out when you are calm. In other words, do not be a sucker for the child's provocative, annoying behavior.

Remember, though: children do need and must have considerable attention. Spend time with the child when he is behaving well. Play with him, talk with him, show your affection, take him on excursions, have a family playtime.

V | SPECIAL PROBLEMS

In this part of the book we shall take up a variety of special problems, some quite common, like dawdling, and some relatively uncommon, such as bowel and bladder control. What they all have in common is that they are highly resistant to change. But if parents follow our general theory and practice, these relatively resistant problems will yield.

Many parents feel that children misbehave because they do not feel loved and that if the child's emotions are worked on through loving, praising, caring, tender mothering, and the like, the problems will vanish. While we agree that problem behavior can be tackled in this manner and that parents, even if they use logical and natural consequences, should always be loving—and have said so in this book over and over again—we do not think that a lack of love causes these problems or that giving a child more love will erase them.

We believe that the best way for parents to solve these problems is to operate in a strictly logical manner—to refuse to be victimized by children. One action can be worth a thousand words. Tell a child a hundred times that you want her to walk beside you—and she may not. But let her get lost once as a result of walking away from you—and she is likely thenceforth to stick with you like a shadow.

25 | *Dawdling*

The DiSanto family was eating breakfast. Jimmy took only occasional bites, and he sat with his meal in front of him long after the others had finished. Mother urged, "Hurry up, you'll be late for school." Jimmy didn't appear to hear. Mother then suggested that Father do something about the matter, but Father did not know what to do other than to scold and threaten a spanking. And Jimmy continued to dawdle at meals.

DISCUSSION

Procrastination, postponing, and not meeting one's obligations on time are other examples of dawdling. We usually consider it to be a fault of character. We all know people who miss appointments, who forget to do what they are supposed to do. Many have been dawdlers since childhood.

A parent who permits a child to get away with such behavior is delinquent himself. The child should be trained to be considerate of others and to finish whatever he does within a reasonable length of time.

SOLUTION

1. When you and your child are calm, explain to him (just this once) what you intend to do about his dawdling. Thereafter do as you have said you would but do not explain again.
2. If the child is *slow in eating*, remove all plates, *including his*, when everyone else has finished. Do not give him food between meals. He will be hungry and eat faster if he does not get a "payoff" of much attention for dawdling.
3. If the child is *slow in dressing,* go out without him. If you do not believe that he can be left alone, put him and his clothes in the car or bus. He can dress himself en route or when he arrives at his destination.

SOLUTION APPLIED TO THE DI SANTO FAMILY

Mother told Jimmy that from now on she would remove his plate when she removed the others from the table. The first morning, Jimmy objected: "I'm hungry; you don't want me to eat." Mother seemed deaf; she did not respond. "You don't care if I starve," cried Jimmy. Mother did not answer but went on washing the dishes. She had to remove Jimmy's plate at only two subsequent meals—thereafter he ate as fast as the others in the family.

FURTHER EXAMPLES

John was a dawdler to an incredible degree, and he drove the rest of the family wild. Finally, the parents consulted a counselor and decided to follow the procedures we recommend. They had the prescribed discussion with the child, and he did begin to hurry up a bit. Not long thereafter, the whole family decided to go to the beach. Everyone agreed to be ready at 10 A.M.

The next day at nine-fifty, everyone was hurrying and scurrying, making sandwiches, packing clothes, food, and games, getting the car filled—except John, who was calmly reading the Sunday paper in his pajamas. At nine fifty-five, he was still engrossed in the comics, apparently oblivious to the tumult about him. At nine fifty-nine everyone was in the car, and at ten o'clock precisely, Father turned the key to start the car.

"We can't go without John," Mother announced flatly. "We can't leave an eight-year-old child home alone all day."

"But we told John that if he dawdled we would go without him," Father said. "No matter that he isn't dressed. We're taking him just as he is!" With this, Father ran back into the house. No John in sight! Father ran through the house and heard the shower going. He tore open the door of the bathroom, turned off the shower, grabbed John by the wrist, and dragged him, naked and dripping, to the car, where he shoved him in the back and started off.

John spent the rest of the day in the back seat of the car with his hands in his lap.

Pete was a very slow eater (he did practically everything at a snail's pace). The counselor advised Mother to tell him that she would give him exactly fifteen minutes to eat and that if he hadn't finished in that time he would not be given anything else to eat until the next meal. At the next meal, he had taken only three fork-fuls of food at the end of fifteen minutes. By the end of the third day, he was eating as fast as anyone else at the table.

Lena was always late for school because she took so much time dressing. Her impatient father invariably had to wait in the car to take her. From home to school was about a twenty-minute walk. Father finally consulted a counselor and took the latter's advice: he simply told Lena that if she wasn't ready by eight-ten, he would leave—and he did. Lena had to walk to school and was even later than usual. Three or four treatments of this sort completely changed her. Subsequently she was right on time.

Tony wanted to go to the movies and his parents agreed to take him. They mentioned that they would leave at seven-fifteen. When seven-fifteen came around, no Tony. "Perhaps I ought to go look for him," Father said. "No," said Mother. "He will never learn to be responsible for himself if we assume his responsibility. We will go without him." And the parents took off. When Tony showed up at seven-twenty, he looked at the clock and jumped up and down, yelling, "Stupid! Stupid!" at himself for not having kept an eye on the time.

172 *Special Problems*

Parents should ask themselves: "What will happen to the child if he acts in this irresponsible way when he grows up?" They should treat the child in the same way that the world will treat him or as much in that way as is feasible—they should use logical consequences. This is the parents' job: to teach reality.

26 | *Temper Tantrums*

It was a busy day in the department store; all the aisles were clogged with shoppers. Mrs. Tacker was nervous. She was trying to find cloth that matched a swatch she was carrying. She had come to town with her five-year-old, Philip, and he had been darting back and forth from counter to counter, with her in hot pursuit. To calm him down, she had taken him to the sixth floor to see the toys. Now she and Philip were back in the yard goods section, and he was pulling her dress, demanding to go back to the toys. For the fifth time within ten minutes, she begged him to be quiet, telling him that as soon as she bought the cloth she would go there with him. As she talked with him, she anxiously looked for a salesgirl. Philip would have none of this. He got louder and louder—and then it happened! He threw himself down on the floor with a scream and began kicking and thrashing about.

Mrs. Tacker noticed the crowd looking on—some in amusement, some in alarm—and became embarrassed. She tried frantically to make him stop. Finally, she gave in and took him back to the toys.

DISCUSSION

We Adlerians do not believe that children cannot control themselves—we do not believe that they get into rages because they just can't help it. We also do not believe that it is good for anyone, young or old, to "blow off steam"—to scream, throw things, get drunk, or tell someone off. We do not deny that under some conditions, such as extreme intoxication or delirium due to illness or drugs, a person may lose all control, but these are highly exceptional circumstances.

We believe that people in a normal state are responsible for their behavior—that they choose to behave in certain ways so as to gain things that they want. People are responsible.

Philip had the temper tantrum in order to blackmail Mother into going back to the toy department.

A temper tantrum is always blackmail done in the presence of an audience for the purpose of gaining a goal.

SOLUTION

To cause your child to stop having temper tantrums, you should, when one occurs, remove yourself psychologically and perhaps also physically. Thus you take the wind from the sails of the little tyrant who is trying to blackmail you. The solution is just that simple. It is best to just stand there and look on quietly while the tantrum goes on; however, if you cannot avoid showing your displeasure, then leave the scene—immediately and quietly. If the temper tantrum is in public, we suggest that you go as far as possible from the child while still keeping him in sight. The purpose of the tantrum is to threaten and harass you. After you make it unmistakably clear that it is not going to have its intended effect, it will soon end.

After it is over, say nothing about it. Above all, don't threaten him if he should have another. Handle it in the same way. Soon the child will get the message and give up, realizing that you simply will not let yourself be blackmailed.

SOLUTION APPLIED TO PHILIP

Mrs. Tacker consulted an Adlerian family counselor and resolved to follow her advice.

At the next visit to the department store, Philip asked to see the toys and Mother did take him to that floor for a short time. She then led him by the hand to the dress department. He did not wish to stay there long enough for her to do her shopping. Again he threw himself on the floor, screaming and thrashing about. This time Mrs. Tacker walked away, took an escalator down to another floor, and asked a sales clerk where she should go to find a missing child. She went to the ladies' room to freshen up, returned to the dress department to make a purchase, and finally went to the lost-and-found office. There she picked up her son. She was pleasant with him and made no reference to his tantrum.

Philip did not have temper tantrums again in public places. At home she handled his tantrums in a similar way (removing herself) and they soon ended once and for all.

FURTHER EXAMPLES

Jane ran from her room to her mother and began to wail. Immediately Mother ran to the bathroom, locked herself in, and turned on the radio. She didn't even want to know what the wailing was about.

After the wailing stopped, Mother listened a bit longer to the radio and then came out. Jane was waiting for her, her face contorted.

"Jane, if you begin carrying on again, back I'll go into the bathroom," the mother warned.

Jane and Mother looked at each other, and Jane's pursed lips relaxed. "Harry was in my room and he took my elephant."

Mother listened quietly. "What do you want me to do?"

"Make him give it back to me. He's your son."

"He's your brother. If he took it, ask him to give it back."

"He'll only lie." Once again Jane broke down and opened her mouth to wail—but Mother was already fleeing to the bathroom, where she opened a book. She read for a half hour. When she came out, Jane was playing quietly with her brother.

In this incident perhaps the reader can see a bit more clearly how Adlerians interpret behavior. Jane was "upset" with her brother but she was trying to get Mother to do something. When Mother refused and Jane saw that her tears and cries would avail her nothing, she abandoned her attempt at blackmail.

Two-and-a-half-year-old Don became angry very often. His temper tantrums were frequent and usually involved his kicking the refrigerator door over and over again. Mother went to an Adlerian counseling center and was told to walk away from him whenever he had a tantrum. A few weeks later, at another counseling session, the counselor was surprised when Mother reported that Don was still having tantrums. Mother, it appeared, was faithfully following instructions—she did leave the scene and stay in the bathroom with the radio turned on quite loud; but Father thought her behavior was nonsense, and he would either threaten the boy with a wooden spoon or actually hit him with it if he kicked the refrigerator door. The counselor asked Father to attend a counseling session. When Father too was convinced that the best thing was to walk away, the tantrums ended.

SUMMARY

You, the parent, must not let yourself be overly affected by your child's emotional behavior. Learn to move away from him when he exhibits negative emotionalism. Come back when the anger, the violence, the excitement are over. Always keep calm and show no anger yourself.

Be sure to give him plenty of love and attention at times when he is behaving well.

27 | *Nightmares– Excessive Fears*

THE PROBLEM

"Aieeee!" The blood-chilling scream came out of Alex's room, and both parents sat up in bed. "He's having another nightmare," Mother cried, and she got up and ran to her son's room. Father turned on the light. Three A.M. He too got up. He went into the bathroom, filled a glass with water, and hurried to the side of his son's bed, where his wife was holding and soothing their eight-year-old. "There, there, it was only a dream."

After a few minutes Father went back to bed, but his wife lay down on the bed next to Alex so that he could fall asleep free of fear. A half hour later, she crept into her bed. Her husband had not yet fallen asleep.

"Wonder what it means?" he asked her softly.

"I don't know, but he has been having these nightmares more often."

"You ought to ask the doctor," her husband suggested.

"I did, and he said that Alex would outgrow them and that we shouldn't pay too much attention to Alex. He told me that if they continued, he would prescribe a mild tranquilizer."

DISCUSSION

A nightmare is a fantasy that a person imagines while asleep in order to scare himself. What is a child's purpose in having a nightmare and becoming scared?

In Chapter 2, we discuss four goals of children's misbehavior: (1) *attention*—the child wants to keep people busy with himself; (2) *power*—he wants to show that he will not do what others ask; (3) *revenge*—he feels hurt and wants to hurt back; and (4) *inadequacy*—he wants to show that he cannot succeed, that he is helpless.

Alex may be aiming at one (or even more than one) of these goals *without awareness* (nonconsciously). He may have nightmares because he wants, nonconsciously, to keep his parents busy with himself, to keep them under his control, to hurt them, or to show that he is helpless and must be cared for even during the night.

Alex's mother and father were alarmed, gave him water, rocked him, and provided him with company until he fell asleep again. Whatever his goal may have been, this parental activity reinforced Alex's behavior—thereafter he would be likely to continue having nightmares and being fearful.

We believe that Alex's parents should not encourage and strengthen his fears by giving him all this reassurance. On the other hand, we do believe that his parents should convey to Alex that they are concerned for him, want to encourage him, want to help him feel that what has happened is normal and natural and that he has nothing to worry about.

SOLUTION

On hearing a child cry in the night, the parents should wait awhile, move slowly, hoping this cry will be the only one. Only one parent need go to look at the child. Without saying a word, the parent should see if he has fallen asleep again. If he has, the parent should return to bed. If the child is awake and frightened, the parent should give brief reassurance—telling him that it was a bad dream, saying good night, and leaving the room. *The attention given should be minimal.*

SOLUTION APPLIED TO ALEX

Alex's parents consulted a family counselor about the nightmares. The following night, at about 2 A.M., the parents were awakened by a shriek, followed by a loud "Mommeee!" Mother got up slowly, and walked slowly to her son's bedroom. Without turning on the light, she entered the room and said softly, "Now, now, you just had a bad dream; go to sleep." She tucked the blanket around him and left the room. She waited for a few minutes in her room before returning to bed, and then, not hearing anything, went back to sleep.

Prior to the parents' change of procedure, Alex had been screaming out in his sleep about once a week. Six months after the change, Alex's nightmares had ceased completely.

FURTHER EXAMPLES

Two families, each having a boy about three years old, were on vacation. At the beach, Ron went right into the water but George stayed near his parents.

"Go into the water, George," his father urged.

"Look," Mother said. "Ron, your friend, is in the water."

"Don't be afraid," Father said. "I'll go with you."

The boy stared at the ocean a moment or two, evidently intensely alarmed. Then he ran away from the water, stopping some fifty feet away, apparently terrified.

"I don't know what the kid is afraid of," Father said. "I think I ought to pick him up, take him in the water and prove to him that there's nothing to fear."

"That's what you did last year, and he had nightmares for months afterward," Mother reminded.

"What do you think we ought to do?" Father asked Ron's parents. As it happened, they had had some Adlerian education.

"The important thing is to say nothing to him about going into the water. Don't try to encourage him, because that would actually discourage him. It makes no difference whether he really is afraid, or whether he is only trying to get you involved, or whether he is only trying to prove to himself that he's a baby. The solution is to absolutely ignore him with regard to going into the water. Make no comparisons with our son, Ron. Just enjoy yourself and let him enjoy himself. And let's see what happens. I predict that by the end of our two weeks, if we really leave him alone, he will be in the water."

So George's parents no longer spoke to him about going into the water. And day by day they noted that he was going closer and closer to it. At the end of eight days he was building castles close to the waves as they rolled up on the sand. By the tenth day he was entering the water up to his knees. By the fourteenth and last day he was romping in the water with Ron. At no time did George's parents compliment him or make any other reference to his behavior with regard to the sea.

When they were packing, George asked whether they could come back next year, and the parents said they thought so. George stated proudly, "I went into the water." Father replied, "You sure did." And nothing more was said about the matter.

Emma, two, was brought to a playground and put on a swing. She panicked, screamed, and was taken off. Her parents were disturbed by her behavior, especially since it had already begun to be evident that she was an overly fearful child, afraid of Santa Claus, of animals in the zoo, and the like.

The parents consulted a family counselor. The latter found that Mother herself was a fearful person—afraid of water, or heights, or high speeds in a car. She was highly overprotective of Emma, always worrying about what might happen to her. Father reported that Mother had resisted taking her to a playground because she feared Emma's being hurt.

Mother was told that she was setting a poor example for the child. Her own displays of fear—remarks, excited instructions, and general overconcern—were reinforcing the child's fears. Mother was told to stop her overprotection. However, it developed that she was not able to do so, and the child continued to be fearful.

Then Father was asked to take Emma to the playground, and Mother was asked to stay home. Father watched his daughter but intervened only if real danger threatened—he then acted, but without talking. Soon Emma was playing like any other two-year-old.

After the Baldwin family moved to a new neighborhood, Ross, four, refused to go out; he stayed in and watched television. He would go out only when accompanied by his parents. If they put him out and left him alone, he cried and beat on the door until he was let in.

A family friend suggested that they do nothing, that eventually Ross would go out. However, after three months of his continued fearfulness, the parents felt they had to do something. They talked to a neighbor—a mother with a son Ross's age—and asked her to bring her son over for a visit. The neighbor was sympathetic about the problem and did come in with her son, Joe; but Ross ran into his room upon seeing them. However, since he was on his own grounds, he did emerge after a while, and played a bit with Joe. After several such visits, Ross and Joe were asked to play on the porch, which they did. Soon thereafter, Ross began to visit Joe's house. Within several weeks, Ross was playing on the sidewalk just like any other child.

At a Family Education Center, a five-year-old boy refused to go into the playroom while his parents consulted their counselor, and instead waited at the door of the counseling room. The counselor thought that the child would eventually get tired of waiting in the hallway, but during session after session the child waited outside, refusing to go into the playroom. Finally, the counselor picked up the boy, carried him into the playroom, and put him down, telling him, "You stay here." By the end of the session, the child was happily playing there with other children; and the playroom worker reported that he played well and was no problem. From then on he went willingly to the playroom.

SUMMARY

One person's reactions to a situation can serve to intensify another's feelings about it. This is especially true with regard to parent and child. A parent's fears are likely to be reflected in the child in magnified form.

Fear in its simplest form is reaction to real or apparent physical danger. But fear can arise in other forms that can be just as hard to bear: fear of failure, of strangers, of being unloved, of the unknown.

Parents should realize that all children have some irrational fears. About their child's fears they should take as relaxed an attitude as possible. Most childish fears do not persist if parents act sensibly. If the child does have an irrational, long-lasting fear, the parents should seek professional help.

28 | *Bad Habits*

(Nose-picking, genital play, stuttering, thumb-sucking, etc.)

THE PROBLEM

"Dan, hurry up! Your breakfast will get cold," called Mrs. Herzog.

"O. K., Mommy."

Dan, four, wandered into the kitchen, sleepy-eyed.

"For goodness' sakes, take your finger out of your nose!" snapped Mother. Dan immediately complied, putting his hand in his pants pocket.

"How many times do we have to tell you that picking your nose is a disgusting habit? No one will want to play with you or invite you to their home!" Father chided.

Dan hurriedly ate his breakfast and asked for more milk. As Mother went to the refrigerator, up went Dan's finger—right into his nose.

"Dan!" cried Mrs. Herzog. "Will we have to tie your hands behind your back? When will you learn to keep your hands where they belong?"

DISCUSSION

Most parents go through the same procedure in trying to teach the child to overcome a bad habit. They usually start with a grimace to

183

show him he is doing a "no-no." Then they tell him to stop. Then they lecture about how terrible it is. Then they try a little humiliation: "Do you want to look stupid?" As a last resort they slap or spank. But the offender just carries on with the ugly habit. Why does this procedure not work?

Our general theory is that practically all behavior is purposeful even though the doer often is unaware of his purpose: Unless the behavior is rewarding, i.e., unless it "pays off," he will not keep it up. But what reward can come from picking one's nose? It upsets everyone. Father and Mother make a fuss about it. If there are other children in the house, they are likely to deride the nose-picker. Surely these are not rewards!

Yes, they are! The nose-picker is given what is for children the most important of all rewards: *attention.* A parent actually encourages nose-picking by paying attention to it. Parents often create what they fear, simply by giving attention.

If you are dubious about this point, perhaps we can convince you by having you make—in your imagination—an experiment. Let us suppose that you consider it particularly disgusting for a child to put his fingers in his ears and that you decide to do what you can to keep your child from ever doing it. So you watch him carefully and if he touches his ears, you say to him, in a friendly but firm manner, "Don't touch your ears." If you see his hands near his ears, you remind him gently, "Don't touch your ears." And if again you see him actually touch his ears, you push his hand away and give him a long lecture on the importance of not touching them. You have your spouse, the grandparents, the baby-sitter, and everyone else also watch out for this behavior. You do this consistently for about one week—and what do you suppose will then be happening? *Your child will be running around with his fingers in his ears.*

So, while you think you are training your child
—to not speak so rapidly
—to not suck his fingers
—to not put his fingers in his ears
—to not wet the bed at night
—to not put his fingers in his nose
what you are really doing by giving attention to these bad habits is training the child to continue them.

So whether the attention comes in the form of moralistic lectures such as: "Peter, don't touch your penis. Doing that isn't nice."

Or whether it comes in the form of: *Slap!* "I told you never to pick your nose. Next time I'll hit you twice as hard."

Or whether it comes in the form of: "If you don't look like a stupid fool with your thumb in your mouth ..."

... each of these methods is ineffective.

Now, what about anxiety? Many popular columns and books warn parents that the child who sucks his fingers is anxious or scared. It is possible, of course, that the child *is* anxious and *does* suck his fingers to relieve his anxiety. But where does this leave a parent with regard to treatment of the problem? Should you, as most manuals on child-rearing suggest, give the child more and more love and security? How? If you increase cuddling and playing with the child *for this reason,* you are quite likely to achieve exactly the opposite of what you want: the child probably will associate all this nice cuddling and loving (attention) with the undesired habit and will become more and more inclined to persist in it. Showing your love by cuddling and playing with him should be done when he is well behaved; giving loving attention during the display of the undesired habit will encourage him to continue it.

We take the "tough" attitude of ignoring the child when he is "demanding" attention by undesired behavior patterns. Give him attention or cuddling when he is *not* showing such habits. You should try not to feel angry, and you must certainly not show it— that would also be attention. Therefore, if Jerry is sucking his fingers and looking scared, ignore him. When you later notice that he is playing happily or smiling broadly, at that point give him attention—play with him, pick him up, cuddle him.

SOLUTION

One could make a virtually endless list of bad habits, including chewing nails, playing with genitals, scratching the head, banging the head, humming noisily, scratching the crotch, making "put-put" noises, making funny faces, sticking out the tongue—and so forth and so on. *The solution for all of them is the same:*

Ignore them.

Pay them no attention. If you give the child attention because of the undesirable habit, you will be rewarding him for it, and he will continue it.

Now, to ignore the habit is often very hard to do. We recommend that, insofar as may be feasible, you walk away from the offender and turn your back to the offensive behavior, doing so as unobtrusively as possible. *Say absolutely nothing about the behavior.*

Funnily enough, parents often arrive at this solution but without appreciating its full significance: "Well, I finally gave up. I figured there was just nothing I could do, so I stopped even talking about it. And you know what? She stopped!"

SOLUTION APPLIED TO DAN

Mrs. Herzog consulted a counselor and then got her husband's cooperation in carrying out the recommended plan.

"The important thing," she emphasized to Mr. Herzog, "is that we consistently and completely ignore Dan's nose-picking. We must act as if we are not concerned—as if we don't even see it. We should turn away from him, but not in anger, and just talk about something else.

At first Dan's nose-picking increased. On about the tenth day of the treatment, he even tried to attract his parents' attention by very obviously putting his finger in his nose at the dinner table. But the parents conversed about the food and ignored Dan's behavior.

"See?" said Dan, trying all the harder. But Mr. and Mrs. Herzog continued eating and talking to each other.

After that episode, Dan quit nose-picking for two days. Then he tried it once more, with no success. And so he finally gave up the habit.

FURTHER EXAMPLES

Little Richard, three and a half, was already a chronic masturbator. Mother reported to the counselor that she had done everything she could think of to make him stop, including putting red pepper on his penis. She was informed that all children play with their sex organs but soon lose interest unless parents show interest. It was explained to her that her fear and disgust about this perfectly natural behavior on the part of her son had made him concentrate his interest on his penis and that if she would disregard the child's sex play, he would soon stop it. And this is just what happened. When she lost interest, so did he.

When Mrs. Jerome stopped reminding her daughter Janet not to suck her fingers, within several weeks this behavior stopped. Her counselor had pointed out to Mrs. Jerome that because the family dentist had told her the sucking could harm the daughter's mouth, she had become alarmed about it and that her alarm and reminding had intensified Janet's sucking.

Little Laurie was a head-banger. Her favorite pastime was to rock in her crib and bang-bang-bang her head. The mother would rush into the bedroom, shake her daughter, and yell at her. When the counselor spoke with the parents, the father pointed out that if he and his wife were in the home, or if only his wife was there, Laurie banged her head, but that she did not bang it when only he was there. He said that he never worried about the banging and never went to see Laurie about it.

The mother recognized that her intervention "caused" the problem but stated that she just couldn't stand the bang-bang-banging. The counselor suggested that the mother go on a vacation and that a housekeeper come in. The mother indignantly refused this solution and demanded pills of some sort for the child. The counselor informed her that pills would not work.

"Oh, what can I do?" the distraught mother asked. She was told she simply *had* to stay out of Laurie's room at night, and she finally promised to.

The next day, weeping, she called the counselor and said that her daughter had banged for hours. Couldn't the daughter be given sleeping pills?

"Laurie expects you to come into her room," said the counselor. "Her signal—her command—to you is the banging, and until now you have obeyed. To put her to sleep by giving her pills would not help in the least to train her not to try to summon you." Mother was asked to take some sleeping tablets herself.

And so for several days she was in a semidrugged state, while her daughter kept banging, night after night. However, on the fifth night, it stopped once and for all. The little girl finally got the message: no matter how much she banged, no one was going to answer.

With Ken, her pride and joy, Mrs. Chickamoto was visiting a friend, Mrs. Luke.

Mrs. Chickamoto said, "Sylvia, I'm worried about Ken. He seems to be starting to stutter."

"Oh, Rose," her friend replied. "I've been reluctant to say anything, but I see that I have to. You're always correcting him. Please stop it. You're actually reinforcing his speech problem. Just pay no attention. All kids hesitate or try to talk too fast when they're learning to speak."

"I know you're a speech therapist, Sylvia, but do you really think I shouldn't correct Ken when he makes mistakes?"

"I certainly do. I beg you to pay no attention. The most common cause for children's acquiring poor speech habits, expecially stuttering, is parents who worry and correct them. The kids want attention and unconsciously begin to stutter to get it."

"Thanks for the tip, Sylvia. I'll try to remember it every time I'm tempted to correct him."

As Ken matured, his language improved, and he did not become a stutterer.

"Doctor, I'm worried about Larry."

"Seems healthy enough to me."

"He's starting to have nightmares," the mother explained.

"What do you do when he has them?"

"I run into his room, wake him up, and tell him he only had a bad dream, and then I get him a glass of water and stay with him until he falls asleep again."

"Well, just go in, check him, and say 'Go to sleep' or 'You had a bad dream.' Don't make a fuss or you will be reinforcing his behavior—he'll begin to have more nightmares and keep you busy with him often at night."

(About nightmares, see also Chapter 27.)

When Hal demanded that the light in his bedroom be left on, his mother said there was no need for that. He made such a fuss, she finally left it on. Thereafter, every night there was an argument about the light. The parents considered various possibilities, including installation of a night light or leaving the hall light on in such a way that it wouldn't bother him. After considerable discussion, the father suggested (1) that a brighter light be put in the room—one bright enough to keep Hal from sleeping too well with it on, and (2) that a little stool be placed so that Hal could turn the light on or off when he wanted. Mother finally agreed, and Hal was given on-and-off lessons. For several nights he had his light on when he went to bed and it was still on in the morning. And then some mornings the light was off. Mother said nothing. Within two weeks the light was off every morning.

Jean, a college sophomore, went to see a counselor about a school problem. As they talked, Jean confessed that she had sucked her thumb until last year, when she entered college.

"Why did you suck your thumb?" asked the counselor.

"Because I told myself that it comforted me when I was anxious."

"What made you stop?"

"Oh, I would have been embarrassed for my roommate to see it."

SUMMARY

Our essential message regarding bad habits is that, no matter what may have caused them, parental attention sustains them.

The child is insatiably looking for attention. If he discovers that behavior such as thumb-sucking, scratching, playing with his genitals, etc., get him attention, he is likely to continue that behavior. In effect, the parents are encouraging the child to misbehave by rewarding him for poor behavior. And it makes little difference if the attention—the "reward"—comes in the form of punishment: i.e., nagging, slapping, shaming, criticizing, and other unpleasant behavior on the part of parents. Attention *is* attention. While the child naturally prefers pleasant attention, negative attention is just as likely to sustain the habit.

In our judgment, there is only one effective way to handle bad habits. *Ignore them.*

Do give your child plenty of attention and love; but do it when he is happy and smiling, *not* when he is demonstrating undesirable behavior.

29 | *Bed-Wetting*

THE PROBLEM

After nine-year-old Terry left for school, Mrs. Huff went into his room and looked at the bed. Once again! There it was—a stain of urine, half dry. Shrugging her shoulders, she picked up the blanket. Yes, it too was wet. She dropped it on the floor, plucked off both sheets, and laid them on the floor with the blanket. She went into the bathroom, came back with a sponge, and cleaned off the rubber sheet. Next she picked up the blanket and sheets and took them to the washing machine. She then went to the linen closet and took out a fresh blanket and sheets. Before starting to remake the bed, she raised her eyes heavenward and groaned, "When *will* he stop?"

DISCUSSION

Bed-wetting is something most children stop completely by the age of five. After that, some children will, now and then, wet the bed, and it is by no means rare for an adult to do so. A few children persist in constant bed-wetting up into adulthood.

Just about every way that conceivably might stop bed-wetting has been tried. Experience has shown that it does not solve the problem to curtail the intake of fluids after dinner, to ridicule the child, to insist that he urinate before going to bed, to give pills or to awaken him and insist that he urinate in the middle of the night.

There are some methods that do succeed in stopping bed-wetting, but they do so only because they "punish" the child. Some parents, for example, use a buzzer system controlled by a pad that fits under the sheet: the first drop of urine on this pad sets off a device that wakes the child. It is important, however, to note that such methods are not as *psychologically desirable* as the method we advocate.

In our handling of problems, it is fundamental that parents must not reinforce "poor," "unsatisfactory," or "useless" behavior. Often parents do just that about bed-wetting. Probably the very strongest reinforcer for children is attention. If we give the child a lot of attention when he wets the bed, he is likely to continue doing it. The answer, in theory, is simple. Whatever attention he has been receiving because of bed-wetting must be stopped or minimized. We must stop talking to him about it, or asking him to go to the bathroom, or reminding him not to drink, or even waking him up. Also, we must stop giving him "service" for his "useless" behavior. The parent who does such things for the child as making his bed, especially when he is perfectly capable of doing it, is actually encouraging him to continue bed-wetting.

SOLUTION

Our method for stopping bed-wetting by *a child over four* is as follows:

1. Do not take him to a physician specifically for this. In almost every case, bed-wetting is a psychological, not a physiological, problem.* Taking him to the doctor for enuresis may actually harm the child because it gives him still more attention and may make him feel he is a failure if he does not succeed in stopping the bed-wetting. Of course, he should continue to have his regular medical checkups.

2. In a matter-of-fact way, explain to him how the problem is going to be handled from now on, and get his agreement to the new

---

* If the cause is a physical condition, this would in all probability have already been discovered by the pediatrician in a previous checkup.

routine:

a) Tell him that you believe he is now able to handle the problem himself. You will not remind him not to drink, to close his window, or to have clean pajamas ready. You will no longer awaken him during the night.

b) If he should wet the bed, *he* is to decide whether or not he wants to change his pajamas and sheets.

(1) He may sleep in urine-soaked bedclothes, should he choose to do so.

(2) If he decides to strip the bed, he is to put the soiled bedclothes in a specified place (we suggest that this be a large plastic garbage can with a tight-fitting lid and that you place it some distance from his bedroom). Tell him that you will periodically wash whatever is put here: sheets, blankets, pajamas, pillow cases.

(3) Show him where he can find clean bedding.

(4) Show him how to make his bed and how to clean the rubber or plastic sheet.

3. Never again explain this program to him, and stick to it without any deviation whatsoever for as long as is necessary—perhaps a year or even longer. Once you have made everything clear, you are going to keep out of the bed-wetting situation completely. *Do not check to see if the bed is wet!* Have faith that someday he will stop. Your caring, even if you do not verbalize your concern to him, can harm him because he will sense your lack of faith in his ability to stop bed-wetting.

APPLICATION TO TERRY'S PROBLEM

Mrs. Huff, acting on advice from the counselor and with the agreement of her husband, called in her son Terry.

"Terry, I want to talk to you about your bed-wetting. And this is *it* between us on this subject—I don't intend to discuss it anymore in the future. I think you are old enough to take care of everything from now on."

"Gee, Mom, I can't help it. I wet when I'm sleeping. I don't want to."

"I know that, son, and I know that you wanted to go to camp

last year and didn't go because of this. Mother hasn't been really helping you, and so now I will do things differently in order to help you to stop."

"How's that?"

"First, I'll never talk with you again about bed-wetting, I won't check your bed anymore, I won't tell you not to drink water before going to bed, I won't change your bed."

"Not change my bed? But it will stink. And I can't sleep in sheets after I wet them. Besides, Eric will sound off about the smell."

"If you should wet, here's what you do. Take all the wet things and put them in the plastic can I'm going to get. I'll wash them from time to time. Then you can make the bed with clean bedding after you wash off your rubber sheet."

"Gee, that ain't fair."

"What isn't fair?"

"That I should change the bed."

"If *you* wet the bed, *you* should change it."

"Suppose I *don't* change it?"

"Then sleep in the wet sheets."

"Don't you care?"

"Of course I do. What I'm doing now is going to help you become a big boy."

"I don't like it."

"Well, if you want, I'll show you how to do everything now, but from then on it will be strictly your problem."

Several weeks later, she noticed that there were no wet bed-clothes in the plastic can.

FURTHER EXAMPLES

Gregory, seven, would show up very early in the morning in his parents' bedroom, looking forlorn, the lower half of his pajamas wet with urine. Mother would let him into the bed. Father didn't like the idea of having his wet and smelly son between them, but Mother felt that Gregory might catch cold in a wet bed.

The parents were counseled to let Gregory into their bed only if he was dry. They told Gregory the new rule. He immediately stopped wetting the bed. Because of the rapid change, the counselor strongly suspected that Gregory had been deliberately wetting the bed in order to get into bed with his parents.

After a while, the parents changed the rule: he could come into their bed only on weekends. He immediately went back to bed-wetting, but when the parents showed themselves to be adamant, he gave up bed-wetting a second time—and this time permanently.

Penny cried when her mother told her the new rules and called her a "bad mother." She refused to change the sheets and kept sleeping in the same pajamas. Soon her room smelled foul. Here was a power contest between mother and daughter.

Mother was distressed by Penny's refusal to accommodate, but her counselor advised her not to allow herself to be blackmailed.

"How long should I wait," Mother wailed, "before I clean up that room?"

The counselor said, "Well, Penny is five years old. I suggest you give up if she hasn't changed her bed by her twelfth birthday."

Mother laughed. "You mean I have to do what is right, no matter what?"

The counselor nodded. "That's right: you have to do what's right, no matter what."

The "silent battle" went on for ten days, during which Penny defiantly continued to go to bed without changing pajamas or sheets. The room smelled. The house smelled. But Mother was determined not to give in. On the eleventh day she found sheets, a blanket, and pajamas in the hamper. She felt that the battle was over and that her daughter was on the way to stopping bed-wetting. A month later, there was no more bed-wetting.

Joan, five, and her parents came for counseling because although she had been dry at night by the time she was three and a half the child was now wetting her bed. Mother went home and followed all instructions. She showed Joan how to remove the soiled bedclothes and place them in the plastic can, how to wash the rubber sheet, how to get clean sheets and make the bed. But Joan would be dry only about three out of four mornings a week.

Two weeks later, the family came for counseling again. Father stated that he was very proud of Joan for being dry some mornings and that he always told her this on those mornings. The counselor had a hard time convincing him that such praise was interfering with the training program. However, he finally decided to show indifference, to do no inspecting, and to listen to no reports from Joan.

Three weeks later, the family came again for counseling. Joan had been dry every morning for two and a half weeks. She continued to be dry from then on.

SUMMARY

We have recommended a method for stopping bed-wetting that has had a high degree of success. It is essential, however, that parents have faith that the method will work—that the child will eventually stop bed-wetting when he bears the logical consequences of his behavior. Once this procedure has been undertaken, parents must allow sufficient time for change—we suggest at least a year (many children stop within a shorter time). If the child gets a rash or similar physical condition as a result of the procedure, do not give it up. A parent should never give in to the child's demands for attention and service.

If the child is brain-damaged or has a physical peculiarity affecting the ability to retain urine, of course, a physician's suggestions should be followed. Although it is sometimes difficult to know whether the cause of the bed-wetting is physical or psychological, ordinarily—and in this respect our advice differs from that of most family counselors—parents should *not* consult a physician specifically about the bed-wetting problem. The child should, of course, have his regular medical checkups.

Why does this method work? Awake or asleep, the child is still himself, and his behavior—awake or asleep—tells us a lot about the child. Alfred Adler noted that a person's sleep posture told a great deal about his personality. A child who wets the bed is giving us a message. Perhaps he is saying, "I am only a baby and can't control myself. You have to do things for me." No matter what the message is, the wise parent can return a message or two, including: "You are old enough to take care of yourself" and "I shall not be victimized by you." In cases observed by us, at least 90 percent of chronic bed-wetters stop within a month when the method is followed consistently and intelligently.

Let us review the high points of this procedure:

—The parent must decide for himself that enough is enough.

—The parent must explain the procedure carefully, emphasizing that the child is old enough to take care of himself. She must not make this conversation unpleasant.

—The parent must no longer show interest or concern in the bed-wetting problem. Even if the child reports success, the parent must answer only briefly and nonchalantly. The parent must expect success and refuse to be surprised by it.

—The parent must avoid any attempt by the child to reinvolve the parent in the problem—it must be strictly the child's own problem.

If this method, properly followed, does not work within a year, other methods may be considered. The use of an electric gadget may then be advisable. However, it should be used *only if the child himself wants it, and will monitor it.* Incidentally, the prices for these buzzers range from about twenty to several hundred dollars —yet, regardless of price, they all do the same job.

30 | Control of Bowels and Bladder

THE PROBLEM

Mrs. Shea looked out the window and saw four-year-old Wilson's wet pants; they were almost too much for her to take. Only yesterday her neighbor had asked, "Is there something wrong with your Wilson? I mean about his . . . control? Have you seen a doctor about it?"

Mrs. Shea had seen a doctor about this problem several times; he had confidently told her, "Some kids are slower than others in controlling their body wastes. Just be patient. He'll get over his incontinence. There is nothing physically wrong with him." And she had said, "But, Doctor, he wasn't doing this last year—he was using the toilet."

Through the window she yelled with determined fury: "Wilson!" Her son stopped, turned around, and slowly started toward the house. "Hurry!" she shouted. How she wanted to punch him! Oh, she just knew he *could* control himself. He just wanted to play and was too lazy to come in. When *would* he learn? Wilson still moved slowly and Mrs. Shea screamed, *"Hurry! Right now! And I mean right now!"* Now Wilson was at the door, looking guilty and fearful. She gave him a tremendous slap, then grabbed him by the wrist and dragged him along the floor. She noticed feces coming down

198

his pant leg, and this further enraged her. She dragged him into the bathroom.

A half-hour later, a white-faced Wilson was in his room, having been told: "Never again am I going to let you out; you're just a baby; you're too lazy to care; you have no consideration for me; you *can* control yourself, you just don't want to; you want to drive me crazy."

DISCUSSION

When we learn from parents that a child has had bowel or bladder control in the past but is now soiling his pants, we suspect that one or both parents are trying to overcontrol the child. No parent can control a child's bowels. A child who is in a power stuggle with a parent or who feels resented because of much punishment learns that soiling his pants really hits the parent hard. He is not aware that he does the soiling to show his parents that they can't make him stop or otherwise to bother them, but those goals usually underlie soiling behavior. Parents become angry, scold, and punish; this reinforces the behavior, and so it continues.

SOLUTION

To solve the problem of incontinence, parents must first stop trying to control the child's behavior—not only in soiling, but in general. They must admit their defeat to themselves and even to the child and start using logical consequences.

A logical consequence for soiling is to have to clean oneself and to put on clean clothes. This is a messy job which the child will not like any more than does the parent. At a calm time, the parent should tell the child that if he again soils his pants, he himself will have to handle the situation—he will have to go into the bathroom, clean himself, put on clean clothes, and put his dirty clothes in a covered container. This procedure should be explained only once. Thereafter, when soiling occurs, the parent must not look annoyed, hurt, or angry, and should ignore the presence of the child while he is soiled. Thus the parents become noninvolved; the child has the responsibility. He will soon cease soiling because it no longer works for him: it does not bring him parental attention—he no longer gets the service of being cleaned by a parent but instead must do the distasteful task himself. Regardless of whether the child's unconscious objective in his misbehavior has been power or revenge, it now brings no payoff—anger or hurt from the parents.

Parents should not withhold love while training. When the child is behaving well, they should give him positive, loving attention. They should establish a time for playing with him. If others are involved in the training—neighbors or other family members—parents should get their cooperation so that they too will act as do the parents in solving this problem.

SOLUTION APPLIED TO WILSON

After discussing the problem with a family counselor, Mrs. Shea spoke to Wilson in a quiet, loving way: "Wilson, I feel that you are now a big boy and that I should no longer treat you like a baby. You can do so many things for yourself now, and you do them so well. I believe that I was wrong to yell and spank you when you did not use the toilet. From now on, when you make in your pants, you can be a big boy and clean yourself. There are towels, washcloth, and soap in the bathroom for you. You know where your clothes are in your dresser drawers. After you clean yourself, put the dirty clothes in this container I just bought, and then get out clean clothes and put them on."

"But, Mommy, I won't get myself as clean as you do."

"That's all right, Wilson. Do as well as you can. I'm sure that you are big enough to do a good job."

Since the neighbor was quite annoyed with having Wilson around when his pants were dirty, Mrs. Shea went over to tell her of the new training procedure. She asked the neighbor to tell Wilson to go home if he had a mess in his pants. The neighbor gladly agreed to cooperate.

That afternoon, Wilson soiled his pants while he was outside. Mrs. Shea, looking out the window, noticed what had happened, but she did nothing about it. Later Wilson came into the house and stood right by her. She continued to read her magazine. He finally went into the bathroom and cleaned himself. He put the dirty clothes into the covered container, but he left the bathroom quite messy. He put on clean clothes and went to watch TV.

Sometime later, while Wilson was not observing her, Mrs. Shea tidied up the bathroom and threw the dirty clothes into the washer. Wilson continued soiling his pants two more days; Mother continued the same procedure. When he was not soiled, she gave Wilson loving attention and played with him. Father also played with him for a short while after dinner. On the third day, Wilson did not soil himself but used the toilet. During the next week or two, he did have several more "accidents," but each time he cleaned himself. And from then on he used the toilet.

FURTHER EXAMPLES

Robert, Gary, and Don came with their mother to one of our Family Education Centers. Mother said that her most pressing problem was Gary's wetting himself when he was at home, especially when the children were going to bed; they all shared a room, and the other boys complained about the odor. She was told to inform Gary that from now on he must clean himself, etc. She was also told that she must stay out of the arguments among the children. The next time the family was counseled, Mother reported that the problem had stopped—like a miracle.

When she no longer gave Gary the service of cleaning him and stopped protecting the other children from him, the children settled the matter themselves and the problem ceased.

Roger, six, was soiling his pants at home and in school. The teacher got from Mother a change of clothes for him and told Roger that whenever he had that problem he should go to the boys' toilet, clean himself, and put on the clean things. After doing this only once, he stopped soiling in school. But then he soiled on the bus going home from school. Mother was upset. She cleaned Roger, scolded and spanked, but the soiling continued.

She discussed the matter with the teacher and decided to try the teacher's method. It worked. Roger stopped soiling on the bus and at home.

SUMMARY

Learning by sad experience is very effective. The method we call natural and logical consequences can sometimes be difficult for the parent, but it works.

31 | *Morality*

(Lying, stealing, etc.)

"Where did you get that toy?" Mother asked.

"I found it."

"Where?"

"In the street."

"It looks like Steve's."

"I don't know."

"Isn't it Steve's?"

"I don't know."

"You *do* know it belongs to Steve. You go right next door and give it back to him."

Bill hung his head and started for Steve's. Mother watched him go and said to herself: "I just hate liars. And Bill is becoming a liar—possibly a thief."

DISCUSSION

A tragic irony of family life is that parents' behavior may create exactly the kind of child they do not like. In some cases this can be readily seen: the father who wants a brave son pushes him and scares him, and the child becomes a coward, with the father speeding this development along by criticism and sarcasm. Sometimes the process is not so obvious, as in the case of the overfearful mother who ends up with an overfearful child.

Handling character problems is a touchy matter. On the one hand, we certainly don't want a child to think that morally unacceptable conduct is all right; on the other hand, we don't want to frighten him to such a degree that he is afraid to admit and discuss it.

Overreacting to a child's misbehavior may actually reinforce it through giving it so much attention that he becomes inclined to repeat it, attention being, for him, a most desirable reward. So remember: when you scold a child for something, you may actually be encouraging him to do it again.

SOLUTION

With regard to problems involving stealing, lying, or other conduct offensive to morality, the wisest parents are those who prevent their ever arising. The best preventive is a good parent-child relationship—one based on mutual respect, which fosters frankness, openness, honesty, trustworthiness. The child most likely to lie or steal is one who has been punished often.

When the child has stolen or lied, it is best, if possible, to avoid putting him on the spot. He naturally wants to protect himself from unpleasant consequences and will be tempted to lie—indeed, a head-on confrontation is usually almost certain to elicit a denial. Not saying or doing anything at the moment is usually best. Later, when you and the child are calm and in harmony, you and he can discuss the matter. Do not try to trap him or corner him, but do encourage truthfulness (tactfully make it as painless as possible). Practically always you will be able to get his agreement to the moral principles involved, as well as to whatever restitution may be called for.

Angry lecturing and condemning are likely to do more harm than good. A parent should refrain from talking to the child like this: "You're a thief and a liar! Not only did you steal it but then, when I asked, you lied. People go to hell for lying and stealing." Such statements will probably make the child fearful and will certainly damage his self-respect.

SOLUTION APPLIED TO BILL

Mother called Bill and asked him to sit down. She smiled at him.

"Bill, I want to talk to you a bit. I found a toy in the living room and I knew it wasn't yours. I thought I recognized it, and so I called Steve's mother, and she told me Steve was crying because he couldn't find his toy. I don't know whether he lent it to you and you forgot to return it, or whether you found it somewhere and then took it home—but you ought to keep in mind that you should never take home anyone else's things. Do you understand?"

"Yes, Mother."

"Fine. O.K., dear. I just wanted to make sure you understood. Please take the toy to Steve."

A little later, Mother played a game with Bill. Each felt good about the other.

FURTHER EXAMPLES

Marlene began telling a series of outrageous lies about what she had done and what had happened; both Father and Mother looked at one another and smiled. They listened carefully, and then they too began to lie, telling big colorful tales. Marlene caught on, and she began to laugh. "I was only fibbing," she said, and her parents also laughed and confessed that they too were fibbing. In this manner they did not shame her, but let her know they knew she was fabricating a wild story.

"Mommy!" Sandra screamed. "Patty has my doll and won't give it to me."

Mrs. Hapenny listened carefully, smiling at her daughter, and said, "My feet hurt—the shoes I got a couple of days ago are so tight."

"Huh?" the puzzled daughter said. "Mommy, didn't you hear what I said?"

"Yes, I did, dear. Thank you for giving me the information, but my shoes are tight, and my feet hurt."

"Aren't you going to do anything to Patty?" Sandra was amazed. Ordinarily Mother would give her sister Patty a strong scolding. Disappointed, Sandra cried, "I don't care about your stupid shoes."

"I am sorry to hear this," Mother stated, then turned and walked away.

If a child bears tales about another child, one way for you, the parent, to handle the situation is to listen politely and then give the talebearer a complaint of your own—about the price of eggs, the weather, or whatnot. The message is clear: *I don't pay attention to talebearing.*

His parents were quite worried about seven-year-old Herbert.

"It isn't that he's really a thief," the mother explained to the counselor, "but he takes things that don't belong to him. He comes into our bedroom and takes anything. We check his room. One time he had our wedding license; another time, my husband's medals. He takes anything he can lay his hands on."

The father added, "He takes things from his brother and sister, and now he's starting to go into neighbors' homes. We just don't know how to handle him."

The counselor then had a conversation with the boy in the presence of his parents. To their surprise, the counselor did not ask about stealing; instead, he asked Herbert what made him happy and what made him unhappy. Herbert said the main thing that made him unhappy was that his mother wouldn't let him ride his bike where he wanted to go with his friends. Herbert particularly wanted to go up a hill so he could come down rapidly.

"Why didn't you ask him about stealing?" the father asked after Herbert had left the room.

"After all, you covered the topic with him. But what is this about the bicycle?" asked the counselor.

"He's too young to ride a bike and come down a hill. He would have to cross a street, and he could get run over."

"But Herbert thinks he is old enough to do it."

"Well, I don't."

"Maybe you ought to let him do it. Most children are very conservative—they don't want to try anything they think is overly dangerous."

"What has this got to do with his stealing?"

"They may be connected. Why not think it over and see what happens if you let him use his bike on that hill?"

Several weeks later, the parents were interviewed again. They reported that the stealing had stopped, and they were pleased.

"And how about the bicycle?" the counselor asked.

"Fine—he manages quite well. He does a lot of riding with his friends. We're letting him go where he wants."

"Do you see any connection between the stealing and the bike?"

"No—I still don't see any connection," the father replied.

"Herbert knew that you didn't like his taking your things. He was doing this to get even with you for not letting him ride with his friends. Now that he can do what his friends do, he is no longer angry with you and does not feel that he wants to punish you. You have improved your relationship with him by showing you have confidence in him."

Wallace was stealing because he didn't have as much allowance as others in his social circle. The solution was to give Wallace an opportunity to earn money. The parents found a number of jobs around the house (in addition to his chores) for which they agreed to pay him at a rate equal to the legal minimum wage. Wallace could now shine shoes, put stamps in trading books, wash the car, rake the lawn, clean out the pantry, and do other things to make enough money to buy the various items he wanted. The stealing stopped.

When a neighbor identified that rather peculiar smell emanating from Howard's room as marijuana, both parents panicked. They searched the room and found a bag filled with a tobacco-like substance. Their son was a drug addict! They visualized him shoving a needle into his arm, the next step after smoking pot! They called their family doctor, who told them that in his opinion marijuana was no more dangerous than tobacco, although neither substance should be recommended for use.

A psychiatrist counseled them to say nothing to the son but to watch him carefully to see if he showed personality changes or if he should appear to be "stoned" (intoxicated). The psychiatrist particularly cautioned them against talking to their son about marijuana.

The parents were relieved after the interview. They watched

their son for any symptoms, but noted none. After a couple of months, they no longer noticed the odor and assumed that he had stopped smoking marijuana.

Unbeknownst to them, Howard had informed his school counselor that he had smoked pot but hadn't liked it much—that it did nothing for him and, besides, was too expensive.

Because his parents said nothing to him, Howard handled the situation on his own—and he gave up smoking pot. A friend of his had parents who, under similar circumstances, panicked and called the police. The boy was interrogated, he denied everything, the police could find no evidence of marijuana, and nothing was done. But the relationship between the child and his parents was severely damaged. And the boy continued to sneak pot whenever he could.

When little Karen, four, said *that* four-letter word, her mother looked horrified. "Where did you learn it?" Mother asked.

"What does it mean?" Karen asked.

"Oh, it's a terrible word," Mother said. "Nice girls never use it."

Mother consulted a book on child psychology. It explained that sometimes a child will say naughty words just to get attention and that the best thing to do is to completely ignore them. Next time Karen said the word, Mother showed no reaction at all. And the next time or two also. Karen stopped using the word.

SUMMARY

Problems of a moral character are difficult to deal with. In general, we suggest that when a problem of this nature first arises, a hands-off policy be followed (if that is feasible), in the hope that the first "offense" will be the last. If the problem persists and the common-sense measures we have recommended do not work, we advise the parents to see a professional counselor.

VI | BUILDING A COOPERATIVE FAMILY

32 | *Communicating*

Parents frequently complain that they are not able to communicate with their children. What these parents mean is that they do not send or receive positive thoughts. And only too often the reason is that there are no positive feelings!

Sally comes home from school. Mother issues a barrage: "Why are you so late? You know I worry. You should be home doing your homework. You shouldn't be going with those wild kids." Sally gives her mother an ugly look and disappears into her room.

Talking should be reserved for positive purposes: giving information, telling stories, problem-solving, recounting and sharing thoughts and feelings. Parents who show good will generally have children who show good will.

Avoid words at a time of conflict. Being silent is effective communication, and it allows you to cool off. Our suggestions for logical consequences (Chapter 5) should help you discipline your children in a respectful manner. It will help maintain a good relationship with your children.

IMPLEMENTING POSITIVE MESSAGES

1. Accept the child.

The child must believe that he is fundamentally O.K. and that you love him no matter what he says or does. You may not like what he does, but you like him as a person. Just a simple word or two will usually suffice: "O.K.," or "I feel that way too at times." A smile, wink, nose wrinkle, or hug needs no words at all, but tells the child you accept him.

2. Display affection.

Some parents show affection only when the child is very young. We need physical contact and warmth throughout life. Accept and encourage your child's affection too.

3. Minimize competition between children.

The person who loses in a competition does not feel good about himself. It is best to encourage cooperation.

4. Modulate your tone of voice.

A pleasant voice is more winning than one that is loud and harsh.

5. Watch nonverbal messages.

Angry facial expressions convey negative attitudes. Calm down; smile.

6. Admit your own imperfections.

Admitting your errors allows the child to see you as human and indicates that you are not always right and know so.

7. Show appreciation.

Let the child know how much you appreciate *him,* not only what he does.

8. Show your enthusiasm and spontaneity.

Pleasant times together build good relationships.

9. Give "I will" not "You should" messages.

Don't say "You shouldn't fight with your brother." Say "I will leave the room when you and your brother fight."

EFFECTIVE LISTENING

1. Do not be judgmental.

Acknowledge that the child has a right to have his own ideas even if they do not agree with yours.

2. Be an active listener.

If the child seems to want to say something, pay attention. Jerry: "Mom, I felt bad in school today; I flunked a test." Mother (stopping bed-making and sitting down with Jerry): "Do you want to tell me about it?"

3. Try to understand a child's words.

It takes time for language skill to develop, and a young child may say something inappropriate. Mark (age four): "Grandma, Daddy is going to take me to a funeral." Grandmother (perplexed, but trying to understand): "What will you do there?" Mark: "Oh, you know, there are rides, and things to throw and to win." Grandmother: "Oh, yes; you and Dad are going to a carnival?" Mark: "Yeh."

4. Reflect a child's feelings.

At times a child's words do not tell the whole story, and he may not know his feelings. If parents can show they understand his feelings, they have a better rapport. Paul: "Dad, look at my truck. Hugh broke it. He's a jerk! I'm going to get one of his toys and break it!" Father: "You feel angry and want to get even." Paul: "That's right."

Our book tries to teach parents how to build positive relationships with their children. Good communications are vital in this process. For more on communications with children, read more on this topic.*

So essential is communication that we believe our most important advice to all parents is to establish a family council, a structured device for effective communications, to be discussed in the next chapter.

---

* We recommend Thomas Gordon, *Parent Effectiveness Training* (New York: Peter H. Wyden, 1970); Haim Ginott, *Between Parent and Child* (New York: Macmillan, 1965).

33 | *The Family Council*

Were we to be limited to only one recommendation to help create a happy, cooperative family, we would say:

"Start a family council."

People who live together inevitably have conflicts of interest at times. The family council gives invaluable training in human relationships. Each member receives practice in understanding others' opinions, feelings, and behavior. Parents as well as children learn how to get along within the family. This knowledge can be useful too in dealing with the outside world, the community.

We are going to give a detailed description of a family council, for experience shows that many parents who start one do not succeed because they do not understand important elements.

Membership

Everyone in the family, whether it be a two-person family (such as mother and son) or a multiperson family (such as grandfather, parents, six children, and a boarder), is a potential member. Even children too young to talk are included: membership encourages them to feel that they really belong to the family and are an important part of it.

Structure

The family council is *not* a discussion around the dinner table, or a discussion while driving. It is a formal meeting of everyone in the family. It has a chairman and a secretary. Everyone serves his turn as chairman. Those able to read and write may take turns being secretary, to keep and read minutes. There are fixed rules of procedure.

Scheduling meetings

The council meets periodically, on a schedule drawn up in advance, such as every Tuesday night after a certain television program, or every Saturday morning right after breakfast.

One of the reasons for failure of a council is happenings like this: someone asks, "Should we have our family council tonight?" Someone else says, "Is there anything that anyone wants to bring up tonight?" And if no one answers, someone says, "Well, let's not have one tonight." Missing meetings destroys continuity and weakens the institution.

Attendance

People are invited, not required, to attend the family council, and a member may leave a meeting at any time.

Order

Order in the meeting is determined by *feet*: If anyone misbehaves to such a degree that the session is unpleasant, any person who is sufficiently annoyed can leave—and in this way votes with his feet! The purpose of the council is sensible discussion, controlled communication—clear discussion, attentive listening. If a member disturbs the meeting, only the chairman can ask that person to behave; if that person still does not behave, then anyone annoyed can leave. *But a member cannot be expelled from a meeting because of unpleasant behavior.*

Procedures

Discussions are open and unrestricted. Anyone can say whatever he wishes, and no one can shut up the person who has the floor (not even the chairman). The council is an open forum with complete freedom of expression. If someone wishes to talk and talk, others can get up and leave if they don't want to listen.

(To have a time and place where anyone can get anything off his chest, with others listening politely, is a kind of therapy, often needed by people.)

Issues

The family council is an open forum for grievances, issues, problems, matters of common concern. It is not so much a means for John and Jane to settle their quarrels, or for Mother to pick on Bill, but rather for the discussion of an issue or problem that affects the family.

The general rule is that any member except the chairman can bring up any subject. Other members may object if it is a subject that doesn't affect the whole family. The chairman rules on admissibility of an item.

Consensus

We recommend consensus. Some parents think a majority vote is enough to settle issues, but majority votes do not work well because someone loses. Issues should be discussed to reach a consensus in the same manner as labor and management negotiate on and on until they come to a decision. If unanimity is not possible, the issue should be tabled until the next meeting.

Purposes

The council meeting is a means to discuss anything of common importance. To give illustrations of the kinds of matters that may come up in a family meeting:

Jon wanted some friends to stay overnight. The council discussed *how many guests could be accommodated and under what conditions.* An understanding was reached about overnight visitors.

Bert asked if he could earn some money doing jobs in the family because he needed money for a corsage for the eighth-grade dance. Father and Mother prepared a list of jobs he could have and also set prices: shoes shined—fifty cents, etc.

Father announced that he wanted to buy a new car. He told the children the make of car he intended to purchase. He wanted the children's opinions about colors. The majority opinion was red, and Father agreed.

Mother complained that the children weren't doing their chores on time, and there was a discussion of what to do. The children agreed on times.

Eleanor complained that Frank played his record player too loudly and kept her awake. Frank agreed to use headphones after 10 P.M.

Father informed the children that a cousin, after an operation, was coming to stay with them for two months.

Plans were made for a family picnic the following week.

Parents asked the children if they wanted complete charge of their own rooms and, with the children agreeing, rules were established for parents' and children's behavior relative to the rooms.

Equality

The essence of the family council, and its major value, is equality. Father is just another member. So is Mother. The youngest and the oldest are equal. Each, if old enough, can and should have a turn at being chairman.

STARTING A FAMILY COUNCIL

1. Parents should make sure they agree on the concepts of the family council.
2. Parents must realize that they themselves are the greatest hazard to the family council because they may attempt to use it for their own purposes, as another way to manipulate children.
3. Parents inform the children of their intention to start a family council and invite them to join. Parents will meet whether or not children attend. Almost all children will be interested, and they will ask questions about how the council works. The parents explain, adding that many details will have to be worked consensually.
4. A date and a time are established for the first meeting.
5. At the time indicated, the family council meets. Anyone not showing up should *not* be reminded!
6. The first meeting should include the working out of organizational details: *Should we have a secretary? How do we select chairmen? How often shall we meet? How long should meetings last? What kinds of things should we take up?* The parents can give

opinions about procedures, but the final decision should be based on consensus. This meeting should also include some family fun—e.g., a treat, such as ice cream, served after the meeting.

Other points to consider:

1. Decisions can be made that affect absent members.
2. Decisions hold only until the next meeting. If anyone wants changes, they should be discussed at the next meeting.
3. Parents should always be examples for the children. They should attend every meeting on time. They should have the meeting even if children do not attend.
4. If a decision is made, parents must keep to it.
5. Parents should refuse to make decisions for the family that should be settled at the family council. "Take it up at the family council" should be a constant refrain in the family.
6. Meetings are not to be canceled except by unanimous agreement. Parents should not agree to cancel except for extraordinary reasons. That there seems to be nothing to bring up is not a valid reason for canceling a meeting.
7. No emergency meeting should be held unless every member agrees to have it.
8. Meetings should be time-limited—short at first (fifteen minutes), then later perhaps a half hour or forty-five minutes, as required.
9. Among rules that may be considered are the following:

    a) Chairmanship to be rotated in some automatic way, such as by age or alphabetically.

    b) Chairman to accept no new topic until all have had an opportunity to discuss the present one.

    c) Chairman not to discuss an issue brought up by others until all have had their say; then he may come in.

HAZARDS TO THE FAMILY COUNCIL

Some of these have already been mentioned, but they deserve repetition:

1. Father or mother dominates.
2. Parents complain too much during sessions and use the family council to manipulate children.

3. Meetings do not take place on time.
4. One of the parents avoids attending.
5. Parents make decisions that should be made by the family council.
6. Decisions are not upheld.
7. Sessions are canceled for reason of "nothing to bring up."
8. People become discouraged when consensus is not reached immediately.

A FAMILY COUNCIL IN ACTION

Below is an excerpt from a typical family council. Present are the mother, the father, their daughter, Denise (thirteen), and their son, Sam (eleven).

Sam (chairman): O.K., it's my turn this time. Who wants the floor?

Denise: Me. Can I have my own bike?

(No one says anything.)

Sam: Who are you asking?

Denise: Well—Dad.

(Father does not answer.)

Sam: Well, apparently they don't want to answer you.

Mother: Denise knows why we don't answer. She lost her bike because she didn't put a lock on it when she went to the store. She was careless. Father and I have told her we do not feel obligated to replace it.

Denise: Well, how can I get a bike? I need one.

Father: One way is to wait and see if the police recover your bike. Meantime, you are lucky that your brother lets you use his. Another way is to start working. Mother and I can give you some paying jobs. Another way is to use whatever money you have and buy a secondhand one.

Denise: Oh, well, if that is how you feel . . .

Father: We explained that if you left your bike unattended, it might get stolen.

(Silence for a while.)

Sam: O.K., anything else?

Mother: Yes. Father and I want to see an opera next week, and we're willing to buy tickets for you if either or both of you want to go along with us.

Sam: Do we *have* to go?

Mother: No, just if you want to. Tickets are expensive.

Denise: I want to go. Will there be ballet in it?

Father: I don't think so.

Denise: What's the name of the opera?

Mother: *Carmen.*

Denise: O.K., I'll go.

Sam: I don't want to go.

Father: Then we'll get just three tickets.

Mother: I have something else to bring up. (Gets nod from Sam, the chairman.) It has to do with the towels in your bathrooms. If they're wet, I wish you would hang them on your towel racks and not just drop them on the floor.

Denise: I wish you would get all my towels one color and Sam's another color.

Mother: I think that's a good idea. Pink for you and blue for Sam.

Sam: I want brown, not blue.

Mother: Fine. I'll get brown ones for you.

Father: Can I have the floor? (Sam nods.) Somebody has been smoking cigarettes in the house. I found some butts in the garbage can one day. You know how Mother and I feel about it.

Denise: It wasn't me.

Sam: Well, it wasn't me.

Father: Whoever it was, you know Mother and I don't want any cigarette smoking in the house. If you want to ruin your health, don't do it in this house. (Kids nod in agreement.)

Sam: Anyone want to take up anything else? (Waits to see.) O.K. Then I have a beef I want to take up. How come all the kids in the neighborhood get twenty dollars a month allowance and we only get two dollars a week?

Father: Why do you say "All the kids get twenty dollars"?

Sam: I asked, and that's what they all tell me.

Father: How many have you asked?

Sam: Lots. Everybody I asked.

Mother: We don't have to do what everyone else does.

Denise: He's right. We don't get enough. Prices have gone up, you know. . . .

We hope we have given enough of a sample to clarify the procedure of a family council.

SUMMARY

The most important advice we can give parents is to establish a family council. However, do not start one unless you really understand the procedures and also the hazards. To succeed, you must operate in a democratic spirit.

An effective family council will help a family cure itself of almost anything that ails it. Families, like individuals, are organisms; and organisms, given an opportunity, are self-correcting. So whatever your problems, it is highly likely that they can cure themselves if a family council is established and maintained.

One last bit of advice: even if you do understand how to run a family council, and do keep to all the rules, you may lose your faith in its potential if your children try to sabotage it. Stick to it through thick and thin, doggedly continuing for at least a year—and somewhere along the line the children will suddenly catch on to the idea that this is their way of participating in real decisions in the family.

34 | *Fun in the Family*

Many parents do not know how to play with their children and often are too rigid to join them in play. Yet playing in the family is fun for all—parents and children. Play can teach equality, mutual respect, responsibility, and new skills. It can teach order and, most of all, can cement a fundamental feeling of love and togetherness. It's true: The family that plays together stays together.

In families where there is a strained relationship, if the parents offer to play the children may refuse. The suggestions we are now going to make for starting family play will prevent any such rebuff.

1. Father and mother should decide to play some simple game themselves. (Suggestions are given below.)
2. We suggest about fifteen to twenty minutes of play in an evening.
3. Decide upon a particular time (perhaps after the dishes are done).
4. Play the same game at the same time every possible day of the week.
5. If the children look on, ask if they would like to join you. If all say "Yes," continue to play, finishing the round, and then let them join in. If all should say "No," continue playing for the regular fifteen to twenty minutes. If some want to join and others do not,

bring into the game those who wish to play. Do not try to induce the others to play.

6. Here is a vital point: If a child, whether player or nonplayer, does anything that is unfair, or makes a commotion, or gets into a quarrel, or tries to get his way unfairly, or violates a rule, you should *say absolutely nothing—but stop playing! Do not answer questions or explain why you stopped.* As far as you are concerned, the game is over.

7. The next day, at the same time, start to play as usual. If any child wants to join in, fine. Nothing is said about behavior. If no child joins in, fine. You continue playing. If the day before there were three kids playing but today only two want to play, fine. If the one who does not join is the troublemaker of yesterday, fine. If he too wants to join, fine. *But again: if there is any disruption of player or nonplayer, you stop playing, refuse to answer questions, and do something else.* But play again the next day.

8. After a week of play, you should change the game. Play the new game for a week.

9. We suggest about two weeks of playing according to this system. At the end of the second week, have a discussion with the children to see if there is some game that they all would like to play. *Consensus*—i.e., unanimous agreement—is called for. If this is not achieved, you say, "If you kids can't agree on what you want to play, we will decide what *we* want to play, and if you then want to join us, you may." If there is a consensus, the game chosen should be played during a whole week. Too rapid changing requires too many explanations and causes confusion. Keeping to a game for a week sharpens skill, and records can be kept.

10. If ever the children annoy you with demands for more play after the fifteen or twenty minutes, you should just move away. If they persist, use the bathroom technique (see pages 26 and 27).

Here are principles to follow in playing games with your children:

Do not play so as to let them win.

Some children will be less capable than others: permit them to handicap themselves. If Johnny, playing toss cards, wants to sit almost over the hat, that is up to him. But if Jenny makes fun of

Johnny for doing so, and if her doing so bothers you, just get up and leave the game. This will teach Jenny not to do that. Don't worry about unfair advantages. If a child does give himself an unfair advantage in the form of a handicap where he cannot lose, soon he will learn it is no fun to win all the time and will accordingly adjust his handicap.

SUITABLE GAMES

The games should have some or all of these features: (1) be old favorites, (2) call for inexpensive equipment, (3) be simple to explain, (4) be fair for a wide range of ages, (5) have a good deal of action. Here are some examples of suitable ones, or you can make up your own family games.

Toss

Lines are drawn a certain distance from the wall, with each person having his own line. Father and Mother may each be ten feet from the wall, behind their line. Jimmy, age nine, may be eight feet from the wall, and Janet, age five, may set herself two feet from it. Then, in turn, perhaps by age, each tries to toss an object closer to the wall than anyone else. The objects tossed can be slippers, buttons, coins, etc. We suggest colored counters, such as buttons or poker chips.

Boccie

This can be an outdoor or an indoor game. It requires a golf ball and tinted tennis balls. One player (later, the last winner) tosses out the *pallina* (the smaller ball) and then, in turn, each of the other players tosses two tennis balls, trying to put them as near the *pallina* as possible. If one of your tennis balls stops closest to the *pallina*, you get one point; if both, you get two points. A child can handicap himself. Each person should throw from where the *pallina* was tossed, except that if a child wants to get closer to it, he can do so.

Guess

Each person has a certain number of counters, say ten. Then a small object, say a ring or a coin, is given to a player. He puts his hands behind his back and then brings his fists out. In one of the fists is the object. He says, "Guess." Anyone who thinks he knows in which hand the object is guesses. If he guesses right, he gets a counter from the one who had the coin in his hand; if he does not guess correctly, he gives one up to him.

Incidentally, this simple game is played in a different version, with the hands under a small fur skin, by American Indians, who will play it by the hour. Its fascination comes from the subtle clues that are given to try to misdirect the guesser. This game can bore a child if he plays it for only a few minutes, but it will fascinate him if he plays it long enough.

Bombs Away

Here is a simple game, fair to all, regardless of age. The player gets on his knees on a chair (or couch), facing the back, holding in his hand a "bomb." This may be a short pencil, a clothespin, a coin, etc. He drops it on a target, which usually is a milk bottle, a milk carton, etc. The size of the bomb and the opening of the target should be such that the best player will get about fifty percent success.

Balloon Volley Ball

A nickel balloon can really take a lot of abuse and be the center of a lot of fun. The "net" may be a towel strung in a doorway, or a set of chair tops, or even a table. The opposing sides knock the balloon back and forth over the "net." If the balloon hits the "net," the side that knocked it yields one point to the other side.

SPECTATOR FUN

In this category we put reading or looking and, of course, television.

We recommend that parents read aloud to children, selecting books or magazines at the child's level. It is advisable to have a regular time for reading and to have it last a predetermined number of minutes. Books such as the Pooh stories, *The Wind in the Willows, Otto of the Silver Hand,* and the Uncle Remus stories are a good way to introduce children to good literature. Older children can take a turn at doing the reading aloud.

With reference to television, we have a number of comments and suggestions.

There is no conclusive evidence that television-watching is harmful, even if violence or sex is shown; and we do not believe in censorship. However, we do believe that parents ought to join in watching children's programs, laughing along with them. Remember, at heart we are all kids—or should be—and able to have fun.

We have found that if parents give children permission to watch television as much as they wish, they will at first, especially if television has heretofore been rationed, watch practically continuously, but soon will begin to show signs of discrimination, and later will take television in their stride. We must trust children to show good sense. If you make all decisions for the child, how will he learn responsibility?

If, with only one set, there are several would-be viewers who want to watch different programs at the same time, consensus should be sought. The situation is one from which children can learn much about arbitrating differences.

OUTDOOR ACTIVITIES

We strongly recommend beach-going, picnics, bicycle trips, hikes, camping, and other forms of outdoor togetherness. But too much car driving, motorcycling, or motorboating—excessive "motor means"—should be avoided. Give the children an opportunity to interact with nature, and to experience nature's rules. Back-packing, canoe trips, and the like can be creative, character-building experiences.

Part of the fun is the planning—deciding what to do for a weekend or for a summer. Planning places to go, equipment to get, things to do—these weld the family together, whether the project be snorkeling in the Caribbean, a canoe trip to Wisconsin, back-packing in Colorado, or fishing in the local pond.

The basic notion is that a family can be fun. However, parents should learn to use natural and logical consequences rather than their voice as a means of control. Allow children to make mistakes so that they can learn. If you can take an adventuresome, friendly, and accepting attitude, you will have children who will always remember the fun you had together. You'll find very gratifying this statement from your grown-up kids: "Gee, we used to have so much fun with Mom and Dad. . . ."

VII | HELPING OTHER FAMILIES

35 | *Form a Parents' Study Group*

Our last suggestion for a happy, efficient, orderly home: start a Parents' Study Group. First we shall tell you why, and then, how.

The most basic philosophic principle of Adlerian psychology is *social interest*. The word that Adler used was *Gemeinschaftsgefühl*, which means "feeling for humanity" or "being part of mankind." All major human problems are due to deficits in social interest. The thief, the murderer, the drug addict, the alcoholic, the ne'er-do-well, the lazy one, the cynic, the pessimist, the neurotic, the psychotic—all are deficient in social interest. The normal, happy, successful person likes people and is liked by them. They care for others.

This does not necessarily mean that they are do-gooders, or that they go around with Thanksgiving baskets, or that they contribute to charity—although people who do these things are likely to have a good deal of social interest—but it means that they care for the welfare of others. They *participate*. They give of themselves.

We suggest that you consider starting a Parents' Study Group for these reasons:

1. By so doing, you become an example to your own children that your concern is more than just yourself and your immediate family.

2. You will be able to help other parents understand their children, deal with their problems, and build a better family and a better neighborhood.

3. You will get good ideas from others.

4. You will make additional friends.

5. You will get satisfaction from seeing others get help for their problems.

There have been thousands of Parents' Study Groups started by housewives using Adlerian-based texts. Most parents who started such groups were not professionals, had no experience at first, but all of them had fun and profited from them.

A Parents' Study Group essentially consists of group of parents, frequently all mothers, or mothers and fathers, who meet for about one and a half to two hours, one day a week, for about a dozen weeks, each studying the same book. One of the members of the group becomes the group leader, and she participates by assigning chapters to read and making up a series of questions for discussion. At the meeting, she begins to ask the questions, guides the discussion, refers the group back to the book—but she never gives her opinions. The book, not the study group leader, is the teacher.

Such groups ordinarily meet at members' houses or in a church, school building, or community hall. Often, the group hires a baby-sitter to take care of young children while the meeting goes on. Usually, one person purchases the books, from a bookseller, from an Adlerian organization, such as the American Society of Adlerian Psychology in Chicago, or directly from the publisher. The total "dues" should cover the cost of the book, the baby-sitter, and coffee for the twelve or so weeks.

Let us now consider how such groups are started and run. There are a variety of ways, naturally, but here are some possible beginnings.

1. You can inform the school principal in your neighborhood that you would like to start a Parents' Study Group, and leave your phone number so that anyone interested can call you; you can begin to make arrangements. Or you can leave this information with a minister, a community worker, scout master, doctor—anyone who gets in contact with a number of people.

2. You make up a simple announcement, such as the following, which you can post on any bulletin board, say in a shopping center or a laundromat.

ANNOUNCING A PARENTS' STUDY GROUP

If you are interested in joining a group to study children's behavior and to solve problems in the family, please call this number.

(Name)

(Telephone)

---

3. You can mention your intention to some friends, asking them to ask other friends, perhaps setting a date and place for a preliminary discussion.

In the meantime, you should select a text. There are a number of books suitable for this purpose. They are listed at the end of this book, under "Selected Books on Child Guidance." The book that has been most often used is Dreikurs and Soltz's *Children: The Challenge*. Naturally, we believe that our book is also suitable. Parents should examine several of the books before selecting the one that appears best for the particular group.

In running a group of this kind, one person ought to serve as leader. It frequently is, but need not be, the organizer of the group. The leader should read the whole book rapidly at least once, and then should go through it carefully, breaking it down into, say, ten parts, each part to take one session. For each section to be discussed, the leader makes up a series of questions, or uses the questions given in Chapter 36 as they are appropriate.

It is important for the leader to remember that she is not a teacher. She gives no advice! It would be completely out of the spirit of a Parents' Study Group to give advice. She should look in the index if necessary, and then say, "On this point, I think if we look at page ——— we will find something. Let me read what it says. . . ." In other words, she does not serve as an expert.

After a group is finished, usually one or more of the parents will decide to start another group. In this manner, the organizer of the first group may be responsible for thousands of parents being reached within several years.

The next possibility—and we have many instances of this—is that parents may start a Family Education Center based on

Adlerian principles. To do this, they would get in touch with the American Society of Adlerian Psychology for information. Your local library can get the address of this society for you, or of the *Journal of Individual Psychology*, the organization's magazine. Speakers, organizational experts, or other knowledgeable individuals located in your area may be arranged for, or if no one is available close by, information can be mailed to you.

There are several dozen Adlerian Family Education Centers in the United States and Canada, so the possibility is strong that there will be some expertise in your immediate vicinity. These centers can do a number of things:

1. Arrange for informational meetings to parents.
2. Speak at PTAs, women's groups, service groups.
3. Coordinate Parents' Study Groups.
4. Actually do public family counseling (using a certified counselor).
5. Arrange for TV showing of Adlerian family counseling films.

Most of these centers operate at very low cost, generally meeting in church, school, or social organization buildings. They usually charge annual dues, sell books, have fund drives to maintain themselves. Usually no one pays for services and no one gets paid for services. If the organization gets very large, a paid administrator can be hired. We have seen a number of such Family Education Centers start out of the humble beginning of a Parents' Study Group.

For all the reasons we have explained, we strongly suggest that the readers of this book consider calling a group of parents together to study this book or one of the books suggested. Not only would you be helping others in difficulty, but you would be helping yourselves due to the power of the group, which clarifies, intensifies, and facilitates the messages within these Adlerian books.

36 | Study Group Leader's Guide— Review Questions

To help facilitate leading a study group, we suggest the following basic questions for a ten-session Parents' Study Group. Of course, the study leader as well as other members may wish to propose other questions.

SESSION 1

Our Ideal Family

1. What would be your idea of an ideal family?
2. What problems have you noticed in families?
3. What are some basic concepts of Adlerians relative to family relationships?
4. What is the implication of our quotation from Leo Tolstoy?
5. Which is more important in directing a family: respect or love?
6. On pages ————, some behaviors of parents toward children are mentioned. Do you agree that each is disrespectful?
7. What are the four R's? Do you see them all as important? If you were to select four words, what would they be?

Fundamental Factors in Child Development

1. Are all first-born children alike?
2. Is the desire for competence innate?
3. What is the reason for the importance of social interest?
4. What are Dreikurs' four goals of children's misbehavior?
5. What is one way a parent can tell which goal a child may be pursuing in his misbehavior?
6. How can a baby cooperate in the family?

Democracy: Rewards and Punishments

1. Should a family be authoritarian or democratic; what other style may be best?
2. In what ways are parents and children equals? Can unequals be equal?
3. Why don't rewards and punishments work?
4. Under what conditions can "punishment" become a "reward"?
5. Give examples of logical consequences.
6. Give examples of natural consequences.
7. Give some examples of appropriate and inappropriate use of the bathroom technique.
8. Give some discouraging and encouraging statements.
9. Differentiate between praise and encouragement.

Consequences, Encouragement, Rules

1. What is the difference between natural and logical consequences?
2. What is the difference between consequences and punishment?
3. Why is the child always given a choice when parents use logical consequences?
4. Why must we be cautious in allowing the child to experience natural consequences?
5. Why do we have so many discouraged children in our society?

6. What does encouragement do for a child?
7. Distinguish between praise and encouragement.
8. Discuss the difference in emphasizing the deed or the doer.
9. In what other ways can you encourage your child?
10. Why should parents be consistent?
11. Why should training be done in silence?

SESSION 5

Problems of Routine Living

1. What would be the ideal technique for handling *awakening* for school-age children?
2. Marilyn, age ten, wants to wear a party dress to a picnic. What should parents do if, after they tell the child that the clothing is inappropriate, she insists?
3. Why are there so many children who are problem eaters?
4. What logical consequences could a parent use if a child smelled bad because he didn't bathe?
5. Of all the advice we give, one we are most emphatic about is that parents should not interfere in children's schoolwork. Why do most parents oppose this advice?
6. How can parents best know the amount of sleep a child really needs?

SESSION 6

Problems of Order and Cooperation

1. What is the importance of order in the family?
2. Define "conformance to reasonable rules."
3. Differentiate between chores, jobs to earn money, one's own responsibilities.
4. Do parents have a right to establish the level of clutter allowed in the home?
5. Why should a sloppy child be permitted to keep his own room as he desires?
6. Grandmother sends Billy one hundred dollars for his birthday and he says that he wants to spend it all on candy. What would be the best way of handling this problem?

SESSION 7

Interaction Problems

1. Why is fighting between children the most annoying problem reported by parents?
2. Why should fighting in the car be a special concern for parents?
3. At his birthday party, little Percival, age four, fights with other children, doesn't want to let them play with his toys, and carries on at the top of his lungs. What should the parents do?
4. At the playground, Sammy starts throwing sand at other children. What should his mother do?
5. Why should parents not select or censor their children's friends?
6. What would you say to a friend who complained that her child interfered in her conversations with others?

SESSION 8

Special Problems

1. Why do some children constantly dawdle?
2. Why do we suggest that parents move away from a child's temper tantrums?
3. What are the general instructions for handling fears?
4. Explain why trying to get a child to give up a bad habit may have the opposite effect.
5. Why do we insist that a child who bed-wets should become responsible for taking care of his bed?
6. Handling problems of soiling are best done through the use of logical and natural consequences. Please explain.
7. Jimmy, age four, starts to steal. Give as many explanations as possible for this behavior.

SESSION 9

Building a Cooperative Family

1. How do parents and children differ in communicating in a democratic and in an authoritarian family?
2. What is the earliest age at which a child can participate in the family council?

3. What is the difference between a majority and consensus? Why is the latter preferable?
4. Why is a family council the single most important step in creating a happy family?
5. Why do we recommend that parents stop playing with all the children if only one child acts up in family playtime?

SESSION 10

Review and Overview

1. What have you learned that is really new?
2. What in this book do you most strongly disagree with?
3. What in this book did you think was most important?
4. Have you yourself tried anything new in your family?
5. What are the major differences, as you see them, between the Adlerian mode of parenting and that recommended by others?
6. At this point, have you changed any of your ideas?
7. If there are conflicts about parenting philosophies and strategies, how can they be resolved? How can parents know what is the right thing to do?

Selected Books on
Child Guidance

ADLERIAN BOOKS

Adler, Alfred. *Guiding the Child*. New York: Greenberg, 1930. This book, now in its fifth decade, sets out the basic philosophy found in *The Practical Parent*.

——. *Understanding Human Nature*. New York: Greenberg, 1927. This is probably the best known and the most useful of Adler's books for general understanding of his theories.

Beecher, Willard, and Beecher, Marguerite. *Parents on the Run*. New York: Julian Press, 1955. The Beechers, Adlerians, operated a family counseling service in New York for many years and give their prescriptions in amusing style.

Dinkmeyer, Don, and McKay, Gary. *Raising a Responsible Child*. New York: Simon and Schuster, 1973. A popularly written book, using Adlerian concepts.

Dreikurs, Rudolph. *An Introduction to Individual Psychology*. London: Kegan Paul, 1935. Dreikurs, Adler's major American disciple, presents Adler's theory in simple language.

——. *The Challenge of Parenthood*. Rev. ed. New York: Duell, Sloan & Pearce, 1958. This is the textbook from which we were taught by Dreikurs. It is a classic, well worth the reader's attention, and we recommend it highly. It is suitable for use by mothers' study groups.

Dreikurs, Rudolph, Corsini, Raymond J., Lowe, Ray, and Sonste-gard, Manford. *Adlerian Family Counseling.* Eugene, Ore: University of Oregon Press, 1959. This book is directed to professional people interested in starting an Adlerian family counseling center.

Dreikurs, Rudolph, Gould, Shirley, and Corsini, Raymond J. *Family Council.* Chicago: Regnery, 1974. A fairly complete exposition of the principles, methods, and purposes of family councils, with extensive examples of family councils in action.

Dreikurs, Rudolph, and Grey, Loren. *A Parents' Guide to Child Discipline.* New York: Hawthorn Books, 1970. Many good examples are given of Adlerian approaches to problems of child discipline.

Dreikurs, Rudolph, and Soltz, Vicki. *Children: The Challenge.* New York: Duell, Sloan & Pearce, 1964. This book is considerably easier than *The Challenge of Parenthood.* It is very popular and is used extensively in Parent Study Groups. We highly recommend it.

Grey, Loren. *Discipline Without Tyranny.* New York: Hawthorn Books, 1972. Discusses child training from the Adlerian point of view for the first five years of life.

Painter, Genevieve. *Teach Your Baby.* New York: Simon and Schuster, 1971. A suggested program of simple daily activities for infants and small children designed to develop learning abilities.

Rigney, Kleona, and Corsini, Raymond. "The Family Council" (pamphlet). Chicago: Rudolf Dreikurs Unit of the Family Education Association, 1970. This eight-page pamphlet is a condensed summary of the principles and procedures of having a family council.

NON-ADLERIAN CHILD GUIDANCE BOOKS

We know from experience that some parents have a hard time accepting our Adlerian point of view. For those who may wish to learn of other approaches to handling children, we suggest the following:

Frank, Mary, and Frank, Lawrence K. *How to Help Your Child in School.* These authors take a position different from ours in reference to school and home problems.

Ginott, Haim. *Between Parent and Child.* New York: Macmillan, 1965. A very popular book. Ginott's common-sense advice is acceptable to many parents.

Gordon, Thomas. *Parent Effectiveness Training.* New York: Peter H. Wyden, 1970. This book emphasizes the nondirective approach pioneered by Carl Rogers, and is almost entirely devoted to effective communication between parents and children.

Gruenberg, Sidonie M. *The Parents' Guide to Everyday Problems of Boys and Girls.* New York: Random House, 1958. An excellent general text. We have a systematic difference with this author, but we recommend the book to parents who will not accept our Adlerian approach.

Mulac, Margaret. *Fun and Games.* New York: Harper, 1956. One of the best books of its type, giving all sorts of things that parents and children can do together, as well as a number of activities strictly for children.

Neisser, Edith G. *Brothers and Sisters.* New York: Harper, 1951. This book discusses conflicts in the family from a point of view different from ours. Many examples of problems and their solutions are provided.

Satir, Virginia. *People Making.* Palo Alto, Calif.: Science and Behavior Books. A solid book, aimed essentially at helping children to develop a sense of self-worth and autonomy.

Index

75 76 77 78 79 10 9 8 7 6 5 4 3 2 1